AF386313

NORMANDY THE BOCAGE TO BELSEN

Bow and Arrow Man by Sven Berlin, 1994

NORMANDY THE BOCAGE TO BELSEN

THE MEMOIRS OF LIEUTENANT COLONEL HARRY MAINWARING MC

JES MAINWARING

Pen & Sword

MILITARY

AN IMPRINT OF PEN & SWORD BOOKS LTD.
YORKSHIRE – PHILADELPHIA

First published in Great Britain in 2026 by
PEN AND SWORD MILITARY
An imprint of
Pen & Sword Books Limited
Yorkshire – Philadelphia

Typeset in Times New Roman 12/17 by
SJmagic DESIGN SERVICES, India.
Printed and bound in the UK by CPI Group (UK) Ltd.

The Publisher's authorised representative in the EU for product safety is Authorised Rep Compliance Ltd., Ground Floor, 71 Lower Baggot Street, Dublin D02 P593, Ireland.
www.arccompliance.com

For a complete list of Pen & Sword titles please contact
PEN & SWORD BOOKS LIMITED
George House, Units 12 & 13, Beevor Street, Off Pontefract Road,
Barnsley, South Yorkshire, S71 1HN, England
E-mail: enquiries@pen-and-sword.co.uk
Website: www.pen-and-sword.co.uk

or

PEN AND SWORD BOOKS
1950 Lawrence Rd, Havertown, PA 19083, USA
E-mail: uspen-and-sword@casematepublishers.com
Website: www.penandswordbooks.com

For
Simon
&
Guy
Henry
Jack
Rosie
William
and their children
and their children's children
the reasons why

CONTENTS

CONTENTS

FOREWORD

I was born Harry Mainwaring's second son into the post-war world of 1949, four years after the end of the Second World War. There was still rationing, and concentrated orange juice was distributed in small blue glass bottles to young children by the fledgling National Health Service to compensate for the absence of fresh fruit. To those who had lived through 'The War' and fought throughout the world, the dreadful events they had witnessed were not even memory. Four years is no time at all. It still felt like only the day before yesterday.

Once my father was demobilised in 1946 he returned to Queens' College, Cambridge to complete his degree. He now felt his wartime experiences were not compatible with his earlier intention to read Theology and become a clergyman, so he read Economics instead.

Harry had grown up in Manchester during the economic depression of the 1920s and beyond, and seen its devastating effects on ordinary people. He and our mother Peggy determined to provide for their children in the surest way they could envisage of sustaining the children's long-term security. To them this meant procuring the best education available, whatever the cost.

After university, Harry spent some time at Marshall's in Cambridge, where aircraft parts and heavy vehicles were completed. His general optimism and new-found grasp of the workings of commerce and industry led to conflict on an issue I think was rather typical of Harry Mainwaring. He developed what he believed to be a viable plan to reorganise processes rather than lay off the significant number of paint shop employees targeted for redundancy. He believed in a duty to create a better world. He had seen enough of the other option. He said if his plan was not adopted and the lay-offs went ahead he would leave the company. It wasn't and he did. I know this because many years later, when I was 17 years old, I was allowed to buy petrol on his account at the Marshall's town centre garage. When I mentioned my father's account the elderly gentleman who worked the pumps, a long-standing Marshall's employee, told me the story. Harry only ever mentioned these events to me once, in typically understated terms.

However, this highlighted the insecurities of life in the UK's post-war 1950s economy and, with the aim of achieving long-term family security, Harry decided to re-join the army on the promise of the rank of major in the Royal Army Education Corps. The prospect appeared secure, adequately paid and significantly more peaceful than the first time. He was disappointed to find that only a few months later, in 1950, he, along with the corps' other decorated officer, was dispatched to Korea for two years to do their bit all over again. His army career continued until he retired as a lieutenant colonel from the Regular Commissions Board aged 50 and moved to the Cambridge Institute of Education.

The key to the better world Harry saw in the achievement of every individual's full potential, and after Korea, most of his army postings positioned him to help people to do just that, as did his continuing activities with the Scout movement.

Whilst District Commissioner for Senior Scouts in Cambridge, 'The Major' and his enthusiastic assistants would dream up monthly 'wide games' for weekend evenings amid much laughter. Endlessly inventive and involving anything from string and tripwire alarms to horses, battered Land Rovers, abandoned East Anglian Second World War airfields and snow, the games' exciting storylines ran into the night featuring diamond smugglers, conspiracies, hostages and creeping through the woods at night to surprise people, ending with a campfire. During this period senior Scout numbers in Cambridge increased by fifty per cent as word spread.

Harry always managed to inspire people.

Throughout my life I had heard stories of Harry, Peggy and my nan's war, ranging through the absurd, the tedious, the funny, the brutal. As they and I grew older I realised I was hearing living history, important ordinary history from extraordinary times which, eventually, they would no longer be able to tell. For Harry's seventieth birthday in 1989, I gave him a portable cassette tape recorder and asked him to record his wartime story, to piece together the fragments with which I was familiar, and to fill in the gaps.

This he did with no script, a handful of notes, diaries and references but with an astonishing clarity of recollection. He dictated four tapes giving nearly six hours of living history. What follows is Harry's story, first hand.

The spoken word is for listening, but does not necessarily read so well in word-for-word transcript. You read, and write, things differently. I have taken the liberty of editing this to make it more reading-friendly without changing the content. I have occasionally and only when appropriate amplified Harry's recorded recollections with details he had told me separately on other occasions, and have always tried to do so from my father's perspective.

I hope I have done his story justice.

Jes Mainwaring

PROLOGUE

I was asked to record my memoirs of the Second World War. I hope they will be of interest to my grandchildren and their children. I'm beginning to record these on Sunday, 27 August 1989, one week after my seventieth birthday. I realise that my memory will begin to fade,

and almost forty-five years after the end of that war, very likely some of the events I might recount may not be in as full detail as I would wish. I suppose, looking back, I had a pretty lucky war really.

I'll give a brief summary of my service as a gunner officer in the war before going into greater detail. A lot of great detail might be boring. Just very briefly, after five months as an officer cadet, I was commissioned on 2 March 1940 as a second lieutenant. I served throughout the fighting part of the war in the same regiment, the 53rd Heavy Regiment, Royal Artillery.

I went through virtually every appointment in the regiment – section commander with half a battery to look after, then I became assistant adjutant, adjutant, and later battery captain. In January 1943, the regiment was split in half with two batteries taken away to form a new regiment, and I was given the job of forming a new battery from scratch. This, of course, I thought was wonderful because it meant becoming a major when at the time I was a captain, being the adjutant. This was shortly followed by a great disappointment because on the twenty-first day, when I would have become a fully paid-up major, the War Office posted in a more senior chap to take command, so I had to revert to be a battery captain. It was as a battery captain that I spent the rest of the fighting war until June 1945, when I was promoted to battery commander (major), and I remained a major until I was demobilised in April 1946.

What one has to realise when talking of one's career in war, if you survive it, is that your career depends on the 'powers that be' and where they post you, just as the Admiralty decides where one goes in the Royal Navy or the Air Ministry if you're in the RAF. If you happen to be in a theatre of operations, with actual fighting going on all the time, that's just the luck of the draw.

In fact, I spent most of the war until the D-Day operations in Normandy, in England training, first in coast defence then for mobile warfare, not in action at all until June 1944 after the invasion of Normandy. I suppose you could say that my wartime fighting action was really only for eleven months, from June 1944 until May 1945. I always remember having at the back of my mind, after feeling slightly guilty at being out of things, when Normandy came, these lines by Thomas Mordaunt you may have heard, written virtually 200 years ago during the war of 1756 to 1763: 'One crowded hour of glorious life is worth an age without a name.' I certainly had several hours of glorious life and, somehow, survived them.

This is just a brief summary of my career as a gunner officer. I'll go into more detail of the time spent almost month by month. I think it might be helpful as a preamble to tell something of the background before the war started so that readers will perhaps have a better idea when it comes to understanding the attitude of mind of my contemporaries and me when we volunteered for service during the war.

DISRUPTION

I was born in the summer of 1919, less than a year after the First World War had ended. It is important to realise that most of my early years and those of my generation were spent hearing our fathers and their contemporaries who had survived that war talking of life in the trenches and the horrors of war. It was only twenty years since the 'Great War' had ended.

Most of the books and short stories during the time of my early boyhood really were very similar to their equivalent soon after the Second World War, when there was an absolute spate of war films and war stories. Indeed, right up to my mid-teens, when one was in one's most impressionable state, the thought of war really was pretty horrific, although I suppose one looked for stories of the heroes of the day. You read again and again in the illustrated histories of the war, with their very graphic pictures, stories of those who had won VCs (Victoria Crosses) and so on, so that although perhaps there was this horror of war, there was also in a way a certain admiration for those who had really behaved in such a heroic way in the almost unbelievable horrors of the trenches.

My father was so badly wounded he had walked on crutches until 1921. He had been in hospital for nine months, and later they had told him they could operate to remove a piece of shrapnel which was lodged in a critical position, but if they did there was some nerve they had to cut and he would probably be permanently crippled. His injuries had left his mobility badly affected but, one day, he fell down the stairs at his father's house and when he got up he could walk again. He had twisted his leg when he fell and somehow it moved the shrapnel off this nerve. After that he swam, played tennis, it was quite incredible. (image 1)

With this kind of background my generation were not at all surprised to have to fight another war. All the time in the inter-war years we were thinking, especially after Hitler came to power, that there would be another war in the end because Hitler was becoming too powerful. But there were these people in the government like Lord Halifax who would have given away whatever they could to avoid war at all costs. The thing to remember is that probably half of those who had fought in the First World War were in their early twenties at the time, so in 1939 they were still physically fit and able to go to war. But of course they didn't want to, they'd had enough of it in the trenches. You can quite understand Chamberlain and everybody else doing their very best to avoid another war. But in the end it had to come.

Then, in 1933, for me there came a sudden shock, because my mother died in February, and I suppose with a sudden trauma like that, to someone then aged 13, you really have very quickly to become more adult, because there is not quite the same loving soft shoulder to cry on.

In that very year Hitler came to power. I completed and succeeded in passing what was then called the matriculation exam. *En passant*, as it were, I was the first boy, or young person anyway, in the north of England to obtain the matriculation certificate at the age of 13. Far too young, I'm sure, looking back, because it meant that in the sixth form at school I became utterly lazy. I thought I was so good I didn't have to work hard. Of course, that set my brain at a lower standard than, perhaps, I should have achieved. Anyway, I was in the sixth form when the events were taking place that really brought about the Second World War, including the occupation of the Rhineland in 1936 and the taking over of Austria by Hitler.

Then, just before the time came for me to go up to Queens' at Cambridge, Chamberlain came back with his 'scrap of paper' from Munich where, because of the policy of appeasement, the Western Powers – that is to say, really, France and Britain – were content to give away or agree to Hitler taking over the 'Volksdeutsch' territories in Czechoslovakia.

I went up to Cambridge in 1938, the year before the war started, complete with my gas mask, and the whole of the country was in a state of unreality, because all the men who had fought as young soldiers in the First World War were by then only in their early forties. They had very recent memories of the war, and they couldn't really believe there would ever be another such catastrophe. The policy of letting Hitler get away with everything was therefore understandable. Those who'd fought didn't want to have to do it again.

Although some people say that Chamberlain was a bit of a fool, in actual fact he gained us a year in which we could build more aeroplanes, and introduce National Service early in 1939. The whole mood of the country began to change. We began to realise that this was going to be another terrible event. As it turned out, so it was.

In the spring of 1938, my last year at school, I had been accepted by the Bishop of Chester, Geoffrey Francis Fisher, who later became Archbishop of Canterbury, as a candidate for ordination, with the full backing of my father. And so, when I did go up to Queens', I read Economics, not really because I particularly wanted to read Economics, but because it was a prelude to reading Theology, Part I. There were only three Triposes for which Part I could be read in one year at that time. They were Modern Languages, which of course I couldn't do, Geography, which I had no interest in at the time (though I have now), and Economics – and that seemed to be the easiest answer. So, when I went up I read Economics for that year, with the intention during the following year, 1939/40, of beginning the two-year course for Theology, Part I, and following that with a further two years at either Ridley Hall or Westcott House to be trained as a clergyman.

As it transpired, when the long vacation came at the beginning of June and I'd managed to get a 2ii in the Economics Tripos, the war was beginning to loom. I was, in fact, exempt from National Service as an ordinand, so I hadn't been given any delayed call-up date as an undergraduate to avoid breaking into university time for National Service. In between beginning to learn Hebrew, for which I went to the central library in Manchester each day, in the evenings and weekends I was helping to build shelters, filling sandbags and so on around the hospital where my mother had died. At least it was a worthy purpose.

And the summer dragged on. I went to what was to be my very last Scout camp before the war, in Studland Bay near Swanage, with Charlie Wood, who was the dean of Queens' College, and the old 9th Cambridge Scout Troop as an assistant scoutmaster. The 9th eventually amalgamated with the 11th, becoming the 11th/9th, a troop well-known to the boys in my family and many others, and with whom I later had a long involvement. I helped Charlie Wood with the running of the camp, from which we saw the whole of the fleet assembled for King George VI to do his review, which I think he did every other year. A wonderful array of warships.

Meanwhile, events in the world were going from bad to worse. Hitler wanted Danzig and the Polish Corridor to be wiped out. All the trappings of 'muscle' and bullying, thinking, incorrectly as it turned out, that Great Britain would not go to war with Germany. Then the bombshell came, after all the news of troop movements and so on, on Friday, 1 September.

The Germans had marched into Poland.

CRY HAVOC... 2

1 SEPTEMBER 1939

I happened to be in early on that evening quite by chance, and like everybody else was listening to the six o'clock BBC News on the radio. An announcement was made saying that university undergraduates wishing to apply for commissions in the army should write to the War Office. I had more or less decided that the dreadful thuggery that was going on in Germany under the Nazis, who had now imposed their bullying behaviour on their peaceful neighbours, needed action more direct than simple theology. I decided to apply, and managed to catch the evening post at 6.30 p.m. with a postcard applying for a commission. They had given the address of the Joint Recruiting Board at Cambridge University to write to. I had a very quick reply to my postcard. On a Wednesday, I think it was, 13 September, I went to Cambridge and managed to tie in the visit with going to a wedding in Cambridge on the same day.

I went through all the testing and interviews at the recruiting board and was accepted for a commission and took the oath. I was given my first day's pay (two shillings, plus two shillings and sixpence ration allowance, in 'old money' of course, totalling all of 22½ pence) and was told that I was now a member of the regular army reserve and that

I would be called forward for officer training as soon as a vacancy on a course became available.

I didn't have to wait very long. Just before the end of September, I had a letter from the Royal Artillery posting branch in the War Office (AG6), saying that I was to go to Bourlon Lines, Catterick Camp, Yorkshire, to report to the 123rd Officer Cadet Training Regiment, RA, to do the full officer training course.

They sent me a railway warrant, the first experience I'd had of free travel, exchanging it at the booking office for a ticket. On 5 October, which was in fact the very day I would normally have gone back to Queens' being the day the new university year started, I set off. A lot of my contemporaries who joined the services later when they were called up went back and finished their degrees before they were called up. Many of them were called up after the ghastly business of Dunkirk.

OCTOBER 1939 – OFFICER TRAINING

I had just turned 20. I went to Central Station in Manchester to go up to Catterick. I was seen off by my father, who had won a hard-earned MC (Military Cross) in the First World War in 1917, a short time before he was married to my mother. He was very badly wounded later. Seeing me off also at the station was my father's youngest brother Ralph, who having been born in 1900 had been too young to have served for long in the First World War. He was, however, a cadet in the RAF (Royal Air Force) in 1918 and, of course, was demobilised with the war coming to an end in November 1918. Later, Uncle Ralph became a major in the Home Guard.

My father's middle brother, my Uncle Jacques, had been a flying instructor in the RFC at Duxford in the First World War. He was a pretty skilled pilot and quite bonkers. He'd flown a fighter plane,

I don't know what sort it was, through a hangar. He'd looped-the-loop in a Vickers Vimy twin-engine biplane bomber, which had never been done before, and I don't suppose it was built to do it. He had joined the RAF Volunteer Reserve in 1936 as soon as Hitler had marched back into the Rhineland. I feel he was very prescient and could see this war coming. And as soon as war was declared on 3 September, he was recalled to the RAF and, proudly wearing his Royal Flying Corps Wings, went up to Wick in Caithness, where he became adjutant at the coastal command station. Later on I met him when he had become a squadron leader and had come down to HQ (headquarters) No. 1 Bomber Group at Bawtry. (image 2)

When I arrived at the Officer Cadet Training Regiment at Catterick, still wearing my civilian clothes, I discovered that I was going to go into what was called B6/8 Squad, and we were the first wartime entry at Bourlon Lines.

There were eighty of us, forty Oxford undergraduates and forty Cambridge undergraduates, and I was the only one of the whole eighty who hadn't been in one of the university officer training corps (OTC). In a way I was at a certain disadvantage in that I hadn't got the OTC Certificate A, which all the others had. On the other hand, I had an incentive to show that having been in the OTC didn't necessarily mean that you'd become a good officer or be able to do any better on the course than anyone else. I was still young enough to have a pretty good opinion of my own abilities, which may have been a good thing to have in the circumstances, I suppose. However, the fact that I'd done a good bit of map reading in the Scouts, and had to look after myself rather more in that sort of way than those in the OTC, didn't do me any harm.

We had a very intensive course. During five months we did the entire eighteen-month pre-war Woolwich course crammed into very long days, seven days a week. We didn't have days off then. We did the entire course that the Royal Military Academy at Woolwich, which used to be called 'The Shop', had done before the war, except for the horse riding, there being no horses at Catterick. But we did everything else.

We had very good accommodation. We were in the barracks, which had housed the Green Howards before they had gone out to join the British Expeditionary Force (BEF) in France. And for those of us who were interested in having girlfriends about the place, there were still people around. The Wiltshire Regiment had gone off to France, but their families were still in Catterick. I became very friendly with one of the daughters of the commanding officer of the 1st Battalion of the Wiltshire Regiment, so I had company when I wanted to go to some 'do' or other.

We had the odd evening free when we weren't cleaning our gear or rifle or on guard duty or whatever we had to do. We did a lot of drill: foot drill, rifle drill. We had a lot of what were called TEWTs (tactical exercises without troops), where you have to go through the motions of, say, attacking or defending positions, doing in theory what you would be doing if you had your full complement of troops. We were still taught the old trench warfare of the First World War. It seems incredible now when you think how different the Second World War was from the First. But then in 1939/40 we were still taught the old system – support trenches, railheads, etc., which you read about in books on the First World War.

It wasn't all hard soldiering. We had a NAAFI (Navy, Army and Air Force Institute), where you could go between parades, lectures, gun drills and so on, and relax with a cup of very strong tea.

During the five months we were there we put on two concerts. One was called *Shot One* and the other *Shot Two*. I still have the programmes. In the first one, I took part in several of the sketches. There was one that I did on my own I called *Sam Small at Cambridge*, in the good old Lancashire dialect. And in the second concert, I did another Sam Small monologue, this time called *Sam Small at Bourlon*, talking about the gunner training at Bourlon Lines. They both seemed to go down very well.

We had twelve in our barrack room. One of my great friends there was a chap called Terence Lecky, who had the bed next to me. He was a Wykehamist, and had been at Clare at Cambridge where he had read Modern Languages. He and I were great buddies. In fact I only recently read in the stories surrounding wartime spying in the book *Spycatcher* that Terence Lecky was mentioned in that book. He became a member of the Diplomatic Service after the war, and he became one of the skilled interrogators who were called in when spies were caught. It was apparently Terence Lecky who finally broke George Blake, the Russian spy whom no one else could get to admit what he had been doing. A fine chap. After reading *Spycatcher*, I got back in touch with Terence, and he came up from Wiltshire for a day with us here in Suffolk.

I recall some of the little highlights from what went on.

In the evenings, when we were free, two or three of us used to go out together. We had become pretty close friends and we used to go into Richmond, 2 or 3 miles from Catterick, to a hotel there called the King's Head. It's difficult to believe these days, you could get a grilled steak there with the usual trimmings for two shillings, and see it actually grilled over the charcoal. That was marvellous.

Towards the end of our time at Catterick came the highlight, and you must remember that we were all supposed to be 'officers and gentlemen' in the old-fashioned nineteenth century way of looking at it, when the Zetland Hunt had their ball.

Several of us trooped off to it. I was happy to take the daughter of the commanding officer of the 1st Battalion of the Wiltshire

Regiment with me and had a jolly nice time. I'd only got a dinner jacket and casual trousers with me, so I had to borrow a tail coat from a friend, Anson Howard who, unlike Cinderella, didn't go to the ball. At least I was dressed for the part! Later, Anson got a MC in Burma but sadly died in 1999, soon after I'd got in touch with him again.

The pay there for us as cadets was that of a private soldier, or gunner. That was two shillings a day, 10p in today's money, and we were actually paid with a brown ten shilling note. I loved Spike Milligan's comment in one of his books, "Brown, that's the colour of money." Pay day was usually Thursdays and of the other four shillings, three shillings went to the sports fund, which I suppose was a bit of a racket, and one shilling went towards your fares. So, if you did get a weekend leave, and I only had one weekend leave in the whole five months, you then might have had enough money to get yourself home, assuming home wasn't too far away.

It was a bitterly cold winter. We did our gun drill out in all weathers. The guns we trained on were 4.5" howitzers, which were known to us as the 'split-pin gun' because all the moving parts, which could be dis-assembled, were held together with split-pins. When the gun was taken to bits and put together again, god help you if you made a mess of it, you really were in trouble.

Our instructors there were fine experienced chaps who were all in their early to mid-forties. There were several with DSOs (Distinguished Service Orders) and MCs from the First World War. One thing at the end of the course that still amuses me, thinking of it these days in our far more democratic and egalitarian society, was when our commanding officer, Colonel Waller, a really old-fashioned army gentleman of the 'old school', gave us his farewell address when we were commissioned.

He told us: "Treat your gunners as you would your ghillies." As if, by some freak of chance, you were some Scottish laird familiar with dealing with your ghillies on a grouse shoot. That sort of attitude still hadn't died out by 1939.

When it came to the time we had to choose the field of operations to which we wished to be posted to fight the war, we were given three choices. We could opt for either India or the Middle East, which was then Egypt, or the BEF in France. As my father had been in the BEF in France in the First World War, I thought: Well, why not go to France?

So I opted for the BEF.

For the BEF you were told you'd be given an interim posting, and would go first to a gunner regiment in England that was due to go to France fairly shortly, so that you could become assimilated within the regiment before you actually went out to France. So I thought to myself, more than a little misguidedly: Well, my home's near Manchester, so I might as well start off near there if possible.

So I asked to be posted to a regiment in Northern Command, thinking that Manchester was in Northern Command. Still young and ignorant, I didn't know that Manchester was in Western Command. So I didn't go to Manchester at all. Instead of what I had hoped I set off in due course to Huddersfield in Yorkshire to join the 53rd Heavy Regiment after practice camp at Larkhill following our commissioning at the beginning of March 1940.

Has to be said, if I hadn't made that mistake, I would never have met my future wife Peggy, because I would have gone to another regiment. It was because I went to the 53rd Heavy Regiment, which eventually went down to Maldon in Essex, that I met her. So our two boys might never have been born. They can thank their lucky stars that I didn't know the correct breakdown of the commands in the UK at the time I was applying to go to the BEF.

One other thing comes to mind whilst thinking of the final weeks at Catterick. Just before we finished our course, there was talk of the British government sending an expedition to Finland because the Russians were attacking the Finns at the time. But in the event, although we were warned that we were to be on forty-eight-hour stand-by, it never came off so, of course, we didn't go. Another forgotten splinter of history.

A great thing for my self-confidence at the end of that course after five months during which I'd worked jolly hard, and I think I'd been a fairly reasonable cadet, I finished in the top three. This was very useful in terms of army service, because when you're gazetted you're listed either in alphabetical order or in order of merit when you finish. The way they did it for our group of eighty was put the first three of us in alphabetical order, then the remainder were put in their own alphabetical order after that. I think it meant that I got the posting I wanted, mistaken or otherwise, which was to Northern Command, as a prelude to going to the BEF in France.

Once we were commissioned we went down to do a ten-day practice camp at Larkhill, firing guns to see them shoot in real life, and get some experience as an observation post (OP) officer. When it came to Normandy, some years later, of course, I had many duties as an OP officer that got fairly hairy at times. That's about as much as I can remember about the five months as an officer cadet, or rather as much as I think might be worth saying about it.

One minor point of interest, which perhaps reflects back in a way to the social attitudes reflected in Colonel Waller's farewell address to us, in the *London Gazette* we were gazetted as 'The under-mentioned Gentlemen Cadets', just as the pre-war cadets from the Royal Military Academy at Woolwich were gazetted. All the cadets' courses after ours were gazetted rather as 'The under-mentioned Cadets...'

MARCH 1940 – HUDDERSFIELD

53RD HEAVY REGIMENT, ROYAL ARTILLERY

Then came the time after practice camp at Larkhill to go and join the actual gunner regiment, with which I would, though I didn't know it then, serve throughout the fighting part of the war. I went to report at New North Road, Huddersfield, to the 53rd Heavy Regiment, RA, on, I think it was, 12 March 1940. Of course, this was the time when people still talked of the 'Phoney War'. Things were quiet in France. Hitler hadn't yet invaded the Low Countries, that was to come later in May. I was told when I joined the regiment and reported to the adjutant, a chap called Corbett Winder, that I was to go and join B Battery.

Just to give you the set-up. The regiment had a regimental HQ (RHQ), and four batteries. Each of the batteries had four heavy guns. Three of the batteries had the old 9.2" howitzer from the old Royal Garrison Artillery of the First World War (A, B, and C batteries), and the other (D Battery) had the old 6" Mark 19 gun (also from the old Royal Garrison Artillery of the First World War). (image 4)

The 6" Mark 19 guns, whose wheels still had iron tyres, were simply towed behind a Scammell gun-towing tractor. The 9.2" howitzer, however, was in bits. It had to be put together before it could fire. It had a 'holdfast', which had to be dug in and laid exactly level, then a 'bed', which was lowered down on to the holdfast. Then you lowered down the 'cradle', followed by winching in the 'piece', or gun barrel. When that's all been put together you install a huge earth box, filled with about 10 tons of earth to stop the gun from tipping over backwards when it fires.

I became very friendly there with a chap called Michael Harbinson, who I've met up with since the war and who now lives not far from us. Like me he has become connected with church affairs. However, the officer commanding (OC) the battery I was to go to was a most wonderful chap called Joe Baker, who later became godfather to our older son Simon. He had been commissioned in the field in the First World War in 1915, and then awarded a MC for gallantry very quickly afterwards.

When I joined the regiment, they hadn't yet got their guns, so my description of the guns is possibly a bit premature. However, we had to go down and collect the guns from Colchester, where they had been stored in grease since the end of the First World War. When we finally got them up to Huddersfield, we had to go through the motions of cleaning them. Of course, they were filthy and utterly covered in grease. We had to practice putting them together again. It took twenty-four hours to do this, it was like a jigsaw puzzle. They certainly weren't guns for mobile warfare.

Life is full of coincidences. A wonderful thing about our guns was that when we collected them, one of the guns allotted to my battery was L34. They are identified by the number stamped on the breech, which is the part of the gun at the rear of the piece, or barrel, and is opened and closed for the insertion of the shell and explosive charge.

I only mention this because at a weekend leave shortly after collecting the guns I told my father about these numbers. What I hadn't realised was that when he won his MC he was attached to a siege battery in the old Royal Garrison Artillery, which ceased to function at the end of the First World War. When I talked of the guns, he produced an old 'equipment book' in which he had listed the numbers of the guns in his battery. Believe it or not, one of his guns was L34. So, there at Huddersfield, twenty-three years after my father had been with his battery of 9.2" howitzers, one of the very guns from his old battery had turned up. I thought that was a good portent for the future.

When I went for an interview with the colonel, Roderick MacLeod, a remarkable chap, said:

> Well, Mainwaring, your first job here quite apart from your battery duties will be to be mess secretary. The former mess secretary has just been posted abroad and I see that you were reading the Economics Tripos at Cambridge. So it seems to me that you should be able to cope with that appointment. However, I must point out to you that anyone who is in charge of an army account is a potential criminal, because if you should put any of this money to your own account or use it illicitly, you would be court-martialled and cashiered out of the army. Let that be a warning. I'm not suggesting that you'll be dishonest, but just bear in mind that if you have an army account, you will be subject to all the temptations which come to people who handle money.

A very sound and rather scary lesson indeed to give to a young officer who was just 20.

This was the first time I'd had to officially use my camp bed. At Catterick, as a cadet, we'd all had the good old fashioned army beds with metal frames and a mattress made up from three 'biscuits' laid end to end, and sheets and blankets, all of which had to be neatly folded for the daily inspection. The officers' mess was in a Victorian house where we all went to eat and sleep. Out came the old camp bed, the one I'd had for some years as a Scout, as well as the canvas wash basin on its wooden frame, both tidied away each morning by my 'batman'. I had my father's valise from the First World War, a bit cut about by shell splinters but not enough to bother about, which saved me a bit of money by not having to buy a new one.

So, there we were, getting the guns together, getting to know the men. As a young officer, I had to take map reading instruction for half the battery, whilst Michael Harbinson, who became my great friend, took the other half. I also did a bit of teaching people to drive. Talk about the blind leading the blind. I'd only myself learned to drive in 1936, so I'd hardly had a lot of practical experience, but at least I had driven, and a lot of these chaps hadn't. This was in the old petrol-engined ammunition lorries. I hadn't at that time yet driven a diesel-engined gun-towing tractor. I had to do that later when I went on a unit instructor's MT (motor transport) course.

I had four superb sergeants: Sergeant Walker, Sergeant Murray, Sergeant Jacques and Sergeant Benson. They had all been regulars who had done seven years or more with the colours previously and had gone on to the reserve, and were recalled to Ascot in August 1939 when war was imminent.

The regiment hadn't been formed for very long when I joined. I think it was brought together in January or February 1940. Half the men were territorials from the Dorsetshire Yeomanry, the other half were National Servicemen. Militiamen, they were called. There was only one regular officer, the commanding officer Lieutenant Colonel Roderick MacLeod, who'd come back from a Far Eastern posting in Singapore shortly before. The adjutant, Corbett-Winder, was a territorial officer.

My own battery commander, named Barrett, who joined us a month after myself, was a territorial major and a most unpleasant fellow. He had displaced Joe Baker MC, who was only a captain and who held the fort until Barrett's arrival. I was glad to see the back of him when he eventually left on demotion. He was a garage proprietor at Wareham in Dorset, who had become a 'temporary' major. He was quite hopeless. He was useless at maths, and as a gunner officer he ought to have had some competence in that sphere. He was a bully to the men too. It was the best thing that ever happened to the battery when he left later in the summer.

The only other thing that was memorable at Huddersfield was that it was dreadfully cold that winter with a lot of deep snow still lying. We had to dig out a buried goods train at a place called Diggle. It had been buried deep in a cutting where the snow had drifted and covered it completely. There were no bulldozers lying around so we had to do the job armed with spades and shovels and get the snow away until the train could be moved off under its own steam. This essential war work took us away for a time from our proper job of perfecting our training to be effective gunners with these heavy guns. But at least it provided a rather unexpected and slightly improbable memory.

APRIL 1940 – BRADFORD-ON-AVON

Early in April we were given our marching orders to go down to Bradford-on-Avon and join the 4th Corps. Heavy guns are usually deployed where they can be used to help in a situation where a particularly strong concentration of fire is needed. The 4th Corps were somewhere down in Wiltshire, and we were to be part of the corps artillery. Most of the officers and men went down in a specially organised troop train.

A small rear party got the guns together with all their trailers. By that time we had taken delivery of the diesel-engined Scammell tractors, which had Gardner diesel engines, the 'Rolls Royce' of diesels. And they went down by road. Inevitably a very slow journey, it must have been 200 miles. It took them four days to get there because the trailers on which the guns went were iron-tyred, and they had to travel at 4 miles per hour. Just imagine, in these days of so-called mobile warfare, the guns were being moved no faster than in the 1914/18 war at only walking pace, like the early days of the motor car. You almost expected a man with a tall hat and a red flag to lead the procession.

For a week or two after we went down to Bradford-on-Avon, we were training pretty intensively in putting the guns into action, 'building them up', which took quite a long time. We had a very skilful WO1 (warrant officer class 1), who we called 'Oily Wag', who was a Royal Army Ordnance Corps (RAOC) armaments expert. When you put together a heavy gun such as the 9.2" howitzers we had, it was very important that you didn't try to force anything, otherwise you could distort the metal and you'd never get it together again.

We had to be very strict in making sure that all our levels were right. The holdfast was the key to it and consisted of three steel beams, which were put in the form of π (Pi). The top of π was at the back end of the gun. The holdfast had to be buried to the depth of its beams before the bed was put down on to the top of the two steel beams running to the front. This was followed by lowering the cradle, which was rather like the carcass of a chicken, onto the bed. Finally, the piece, which was what everyone thinks of as the gun barrel, was winched forward from the rear through the slides in the inner sides of the cradle until it was fully home. Last of all, the cubic earth box had to be filled with earth, about 10 tons of it, after being put together on top of the front of the holdfast. And then the job was done.

What was fascinating about this period for me was that it was the first time, having settled down into the battery, that I began to look at the different personalities around me. There were differing characters among the officers, the battery had six. And, of course, there were very different personalities amongst the men.

Amongst my fellow officers was John Merton, who was one of nature's gentlemen, the nicest chap of all. He was a wonderful artist and later became a Royal Academician. He was quite famous at one stage after the war for doing what he called 'mirror paintings'. He'd paint a portrait of some beautiful woman looking in a mirror and would incorporate a reverse picture of her. His wife was a beautiful French woman whose distress was plain when Germans invaded the Low Countries and went on into France. It certainly brought home to us the personal pain of the Nazi invasion.

Another officer was Tony Ryder. I didn't like him at all. He was a London B.Sc. and an arrogant fellow, and a know-all too. He was sarcastic with the men. Sarcasm, of course, is the lowest form of wit, and it's very unkind because the chaps can't answer you back when you're an officer. It really is a cruel, unpleasant thing to do and something to avoid.

Then, the other officers we had. Michael Harbinson I've mentioned. And then, of course, we had the battery captain, Joe Baker, who was a father figure to me. When I arrived at Huddersfield he had been in command of the battery, but was later supplanted by a territorial major, Barrett. Joe Baker was in his forties and I suppose Barrett was in his early thirties and not a good chap at all, not a patch on Joe Baker.

The time went pretty quickly in those first few days in Bradford-on-Avon. I met one or two of the officers' wives. I met John Merton's wife. I met Joe Baker's wife Mary and their daughter Sheila, who was only 13 and at the end of her school holidays. Mary and Sheila had some sort of lodging house accommodation in Bradford-on-Avon.

Whilst talking of personalities, Tony Ryder said a strange thing to me one day going back to the mess for lunch.

"You like to be popular," he said, and I thought I detected a hint of jealousy.

He was intensely disliked. I really hadn't thought about popularity at all. I hate to say it but it gave me a strangely warm glow when he said it, but I also knew it was no use trying to be popular, because if you try it just won't work. The men must take you as they find you.

As far as I was concerned, the men were keen. They responded to showing an interest in them. I suppose I've always liked people anyway and, as for my chaps, I asked them about their families and personal interests. I got to know them all as individuals and the different sorts they might be. Humorous chaps, dour blokes, timid fellows, extroverts, boasters, all so varied and so responsive when you did take an interest and see what they were about. They were very keen on the work too, and some of them became really excellent with the guns.

Some became potential signallers. We had our No. 11 radio sets delivered there. They needed a lot of very careful tuning. I had to learn that first and then pass it on to the men who were being selected as signallers. I'd got the signaller's badge in the Scouts, so I was fairly good at Morse, and of course the communication between the guns and the observation post was at that time always in artillery code, in Morse. It was quite a hard business really, teaching them Morse and then practising it.

The artillery code was a simple coding of letters that gave instructions for the range and bearing, etc., to the target, that sort of thing. Quite tricky initially, to be sure you gave the right orders.

There was only one chap in the battery who had difficulties reading and writing. He was a man called Patsy Crampton, one of the cooks. He'd been an army boxer, full of Cockney fun, a very nice chap. I was very touched when he confided in me one day that he couldn't read or write and asked me if I'd help him to write home to his wife. He didn't like to ask any of his mates, so he asked if I would mind writing home for him. I was very touched about that and, of course, I did. I wrote what he told me to write, he was very thankful. Later on, when we moved into the village of Uggeshall in East Anglia on coastal defence, he came as a cook with my section of the battery. I was jolly glad to have him, he was a first class fellow in every way.

APRIL 1940 – TRAINING NEVER ENDS

ALL ABOUT MOTOR TRANSPORT

Towards the end of April I was sent at pretty short notice to a unit instructor's MT Course at the RMCS (Royal Military College of Science), which had been moved down to Lydd, near Dungeness, in Kent. This was a four-week course. The first two weeks were spent dealing with petrol-engined vehicles, the third week on diesel-engined vehicles, and the final week, as a sort of bonus, on motorcycles. It was late April by then, but it was late May when I came back to the regiment.

During that time, in the last two weeks of the course, the Germans had invaded the Low Countries, and things weren't going so well in France. After our day's course work we were sent on beach patrols. The only armament we had was a .45" revolver and six rounds of ammunition to defend the entire beach with.

Back to the course itself. During the first two weeks we had lectures and demonstrations on petrol engines, such as fault-finding, which was very much more simple in those days before today's electronic devices. Then we had the week with the diesels, heavy Scammell gun-towing tractors. They had four-wheel drive through coupled driving wheels at the back, and two wheels at the front that were mounted on an axle that was pivoted in the middle – so that if you were driving on rough ground you'd suddenly see, out of the corner of your eye, a wheel rising up beside you whilst the vehicle was in fact going along straight and level. These front wheels were taking account of all the dips in the ground. We didn't go far along roads with these vehicles when we were learning about driving them.

We went over fairly rough ground. And, with the Scammell tractors and their diesel engines, it was quite fascinating.

We were shown how to use massive earth pins. I suppose they were 3'6" long. They all had to be got into the ground with sledge hammers, and they were used as an anchor with the winch. This could then be used with the special steel tow rope to get the tractor out of trouble, when stuck in muddy ground for instance. We were shown how to control the winch when you needed to get a gun out of trouble, pulling it towards the vehicle itself. We had wheel- and tyre-changing. I had no idea how heavy they were. Then we had more lectures, more fault-finding, and so on.

The most exciting week of the course was, needless to say, on the motorbikes. I'd never ridden a motorbike in my life before, so it's just as well we were taught from scratch. I had to walk with the motorbike in gear, first on the left-hand side, and get aboard and get off on the right-hand side, and then repeat the process the other way. I tripped on one occasion and as I fell, of course, I hadn't released the twist grip throttle, which caused the bike to roar forward in first gear dragging me along with it. One of the levers, I don't know which one it was, gouged a great tear along the top of a finger. I still have the scar.

Once we'd learnt how to control the bike properly, getting on and off in a variety of weird circumstances, stop and start and so on, the motorbike riding was very exciting. We went across ploughed fields, we went down the side of chalk pits and tried to get up them again. We learnt how to get off going downhill or up if you were getting into difficulties, how to stall the bike. We drove over pebbly beaches and down all sorts of slopes. I can't remember now the exact spots, but it was all somewhere near the Romney, Hythe and Dymchurch Light Railway.

Then more lectures, with more practical fault-finding on the motorbikes. Rough-riding, of course, was very exciting. The rubber parts of the footrests on each side had been removed, leaving only the metal stubs. We stood up on these as we went along so the saddles were bucking freely beneath us. It was great fun. No crash helmets in those days, we did it all bare-headed.

My final report on the motorcycling was: 'An eccentric motorcyclist who should improve with experience.'

Then I went back to the battery, and had a lighthearted interlude showing off my newly acquired motorbike skills. Our guns had been repeatedly put in and out of action for practice in a huge sports field. I thought I would put on an exhibition of how to do anything on a motorbike, so I started by riding at high speed round the field. I had no idea I was heading straight towards a sand pit for long jumps. That swiftly brought me off and abruptly but, entertainingly, ended my career as a motorcycle stunt man. I then simply had the richly deserved job of cleaning the sand off every nook and cranny in this poor old bike.

3

...AND LET SLIP...

MAY 1940 – DUNKIRK: THE AFTERMATH

Very soon after training, we were nearly at the end of May and the evacuation from Dunkirk was in progress. They must have done some pretty good co-ordination work in the War Office, because we had to go out in dead of night to Bradford-on-Avon Station with our lorries with their canvas back covers down. Then in came a troop train with men from our sister regiment on board. The 54th Heavy Regiment had been in France, and had to spike their guns at Dunkirk so that nothing useable fell into the hands of the enemy. Quite a number of the chaps had got away, I should think three quarters of the battery, and we brought them back from the train in our lorries.

They were confined to camp for twenty-four hours. It was awful feeling that they had to be kept confined, but we had to find out from them their next of kin's address and send off telegrams for them. They were in a terrible state, they only had the clothes they stood up in. We managed to get hold of clean uniforms from the ordnance stores, and after this confinement they were sent home on survivor's leave.

That was the time when Churchill was making those wonderful morale-raising speeches to rally the country. He'd taken over from

Chamberlain on 10 May, when the Germans invaded France and the Low Countries. There was his famous speech:

> We shall fight on the beaches,
> we shall fight on the landing grounds,
> we shall fight in the fields
> and in the streets,
> we shall fight in the hills,
> we shall never surrender...

And there was his suggestion to unite with France and become one country. France was no longer in a position to accept.

I said earlier that the regiment was going to be part of 4th Corps, but now 4th Corps was not going where it had originally been destined. We were taken out of 4th Corps and were sent to practice camp at Larkhill, where all our guns were calibrated. A wonderful sight, sixteen heavy guns all in line. (image 5)

The calibration was to make sure the guns' sights were adjusted where necessary to ensure that their settings would be correct for the various ranges and charges from our range tables.

Things moved pretty quickly once we'd finished calibrating the guns. Nationally, the evacuation of Dunkirk was completed and, looking back, it was amazing. There was no panic about the country anywhere. Churchill made it very clear that we were going to fight on and not surrender.

COASTAL DEFENCE, SUFFOLK

The role of our particular regiment was then changed by the War Office. With the rising fear of invasion the cry was 'All hands to the coast.' We were heavy gunners, and it was thought the best use to which we could be put, as we weren't really mobile, was somewhere near the most likely points of attack.

We were diverted to Suffolk and our regiment became employed on coastal defence along the coast of East Anglia. So we then moved, you can imagine how slowly, at 4 miles an hour. It took us a week to get to the Suffolk coast from Larkhill.

I can remember one or two things about that move. We went up that long hill at Welwyn and stopped there, with all our guns and vehicles pushed off to the side of the road under the trees.

Whilst we were there, the battery commander of D Battery, Major Stokely, shot himself.

It was discovered later that he'd misappropriated some of the money in the battery funds, about £30. Of course to do that was a court-martial offence. The colonel, when he had made me mess secretary at Huddersfield, said: "You're potentially a criminal once you're in charge of an army fund." Major Stokely had broken the rules, couldn't face the disgrace, and shot himself. So very quickly the commanding officer had to find another commander for D Battery.

However, that was another battery from mine, and you live in the very small community of your own battery. That was where your own responsibilities lay, and that was where you stayed.

We went on by stages from Welwyn. I remember we stayed overnight in Haverhill. I was actually billeted overnight with Joe Baker at a place called Cambridge House near to what was then a gasworks.

On the previous day we had come up through Cambridge, and I was left in charge of the battery column. Joe Baker and Major Barrett had gone up towards the coast to have a quick look at where they were thinking of putting our guns.

I decided that we should go along the 'backs' where we could at least appreciate the view of King's College Chapel just across the river. We stopped between King's and Queens' Colleges, which form their own part of the backs there, so the battery could brew up their lunch. I quietly disappeared into Queens' and called on Charlie Wood, the dean, and had a cup of coffee with Henry Hart, then chaplain of the college, with whom I should have been studying Theology during that university year had I not joined the army. It was a great surprise for them and a pleasant interlude for me.

From there we went up through Bury St Edmunds, but I don't remember very much about our route through the town. I do remember reflecting that the ancient abbey there had played host to the rebellious barons as they successfully conspired to force King John to sign the *Magna Carta*. It somehow felt appropriate that our guns should pass through the birthplace of the democracy we were preparing to defend.

On our way further up towards the coast, we stopped at Sibton Park near Peasenhall, just short of Yoxford, and about 16 miles from where our guns were to be. During the next two days, all the officers from the battery went to see where the battery's guns were to be put in position. Battery HQ was going to be in Sotterley Hall, not far from Beccles. Michael Harbinson and I were to take our two guns, the right section, to Uggeshall. The left section, which was at that time Tony Ryder and John Merton's, were to go and put their guns into the grounds of Sotterley Park itself.

We spent two very comfortable nights, for a change, in real beds at Sibton Hall. Sibton Hall is a lovely eighteenth-century Georgian house. I remember well the owner, a retired colonel of the Inniskilling Dragoon Guards, Colonel Brooke. He called himself the Inniskillinger. He had a rather good cartoon of himself from the old *Tatler* magazine, picturing him with other officers from his regiment in their mess dress 'monkey jackets' and tight cavalry trousers.

Colonel Brooke was certainly no fool. Though retired, he knew all the rules. We'd damaged one or two of his gates taking our guns through to hide them under the trees and the ground had been very muddy. He charged for the damage and also charged for billeting us in his house for the two days and nights. I don't think he got much out of it but it made me realise that the army can't just swan about the place taking advantage of its contacts for nothing.

UGGESHALL – A FEARSOME FORTRESS

Uggeshall was the place where Michael Harbinson and I were to be for the next four months. We had the very tricky job of getting our first gun into a difficult position down a slope near to the farm pond. The other one we had to get into position near Church Farm.

Mike and I as officers, and this is one of the injustices of life, were billeted at the rectory. The men all slept under canvas around their gun and there were we, each of us sleeping in turn in the comfort of the rectory. One of us was on duty throughout each night at the gun position, where the command post was in the farmhouse, with telephone control to the guns from there.

Nothing, of course, was operational until the signal line was laid to the observation post (OP). I had the job of recceing the route to lay the signal wire up to the OP. The OP had already been positioned by Joe Baker, who really knew what he was about and had decided to position it at the edge of the cliffs near Easton Broad. We laid the signal cable to the OP through Uggeshall and on through the Wangford Marshes and Reydon, to a point just south of Easton Broad.

Since we were there, those sandstone cliffs have now receded due to erosion. Something like 300 – 400 yards, so that the position of our OP is now covered by the sea. At the time, however, we had to dig out this great hole and disguise it with bracken so it couldn't be seen from the sea. Fortunately, it was good, sunny weather at the time, but I still went down to Southwold in search of timber to put in the bottom of the pit, otherwise it would get pretty messy with the inevitable rain.

When I got to Southwold I stopped to enquire about timber. I happened to stop near the old abandoned railway station for the Mid-Suffolk Light Railway, which used to run until about 1929 from Southwold to Halesworth.

The actual station buildings were still there, albeit pretty decrepit. One of the chaps standing there happened to be a police sergeant, who kindly asked what we were looking for. So I said I needed some timber we could lie on in an OP we were making up near Easton Broad.

He said: "Well, how about this then? There's the old lavatory doors, they've fallen off their hinges during the last couple of weeks. You'd better take those."

So I took two pretty solid old-fashioned lavatory doors, each of which had a brass knob on, with the words 'Put a penny in the slot and slide the knob'. I suppose that makes me one of that rare breed of people who have actually slept on a lavatory door. At least it was something we could lie on and stay dry when not actually on observation duty looking for invaders.

Within days of getting to Suffolk, John Merton was replaced by a chap called Warwick. We called him Rocky Warwick because he'd read Geology at Birmingham University. Very nice chap. John had gone off to become an expert with camouflage. He eventually invented the system that was used in the D-Day invasion of having horizontal aerial photographs over-marked with the map grid-lines so that, when planes were flying overhead, the pilots were able to use the photos as if they were maps to help them identify targets when troops on the ground called for air support. He was replaced by Douglas Beaton, who later became my best man when I got married.

There were one or two holiday bungalows along the cliffs which were used by the 1st/4th South Lancashire Infantry Battalion for storing ammunition and so on. Their positions were very widely spread out and this one battalion covered the coast from Lowestoft to Southwold, which must be every bit of 14 miles.

To show how desperate things were, our regiment consisted of just the four batteries of four guns, making a total of sixteen guns. A Battery was near Cromer. I suppose they covered the approaches to the Wash. We covered the coast from Lowestoft to Walberswick. C Battery was at Wix, which is just west of Walton on the Naze, so they were guarding the approaches to Harwich. And D Battery was at Burnham-on-Crouch, way south of where we were. They were really covering the approaches on the north side of the Thames. I suppose anyone coming down towards Maplin Sands and Southend would be passing their way.

So we had the sum total of sixteen guns covering a coastline of 100 miles. RHQ was at Saxmundham, which is around the middle of that stretch.

It was a jolly good job the Germans didn't invade when it comes down to it. Especially when you realise that as far as personal weapons were concerned our battery with 180 men altogether only had sixty rifles between all of us. And those who didn't have rifles simply had pikes, which were really hollow iron bars with a First World War Lea-Enfield bayonet stuck in the end, hopefully welded on. It wasn't very much.

The gun positions themselves had to be best protected so the available rifles were distributed amongst them. Up at the OP, I had a revolver and my OP assistant, my signaller and the driver simply had a pike each.

Talk about *Dad's Army*. [A very popular BBC TV hit comedy show also featuring, ironically, another somewhat different Captain Mainwaring.] If the Germans had been in a position to invade then, quite honestly there would have been very little we could have done to stop them.

UGGESHALL – NOT SO FEARSOME AFTER ALL

Once we'd settled down, with the OP established and the guns properly in position, life became rather more of a routine, getting the chaps more expert in their gun drill and their signalling.

One of the things our duty rosters gave me was the job of dealing with a problem of morale. We needed to have certain jobs covered by someone on duty twenty-four hours a day. We tried to give everyone a certain amount of time off once the work routine had become established at the gun positions.

We had some transport available as what we called passion wagons. We had one of the old ammunition trucks take men who had the evening off into Lowestoft, where the bright lights were. Michael Harbinson and I got the No.1's together (the 'No. 1' was the full sergeant in charge of a gun) to decide which of their men could go off duty, and we worked a routine, initially, where they went, some on weekdays, some on Saturdays, some on Sundays.

However, after three or four weeks of this, we realised that the same people were having the Saturdays every week and similarly for the other days. I never got to the bottom of how they were selected for a particular day off, but we could see that there was a certain amount of unhappiness about the system.

I used to play chess now and again with Bombardier Parsons, an expert gunner. He pointed out to me one day: "The problem is that people don't like always having the same day off. Especially if it means always having to go to Lowestoft on Thursdays. It's early closing day and the town is dead as a dodo."

Michael Harbinson and I realised the simple solution was to ensure that everyone had a different day every week. We decided to give the men their time off once in every eight days, there not being enough leeway to allow reducing the gap between time off to once every six days. That meant that if you had Monday off one week, you would have Tuesday off the next week and so on. Everybody had the chance of a turn at a weekend when there was more going on in the town. Whilst they ended up with less time off, this seemed to work and things settled into a much more satisfactory routine.

Occasionally I had my own time off. I had taken a shine to Colonel Brooke's niece Pamela Darley at Sibton Hall. When I had my free time, I used to cycle back to Sibton Park and chat to her and Colonel Brooke, go for walks round the park, and so on. On one occasion I even went to Sibton Church and read a lesson at morning service. Time passed fairly quickly there.

On another occasion, Michael Harbinson had made friends with a girl called Barbara Saunders, step-daughter of a family named Stannard who ran Uggeshall Hall Farm, and they had a tennis court. Michael liked to play tennis and went over there to play. On one of the very few occasions when we were both able to have time off, Joe Baker came over to cover the gun position for the afternoon.

Michael and I went up together to the hall to play tennis with Barbara and her sister. When we got there, there was old Barrett, the battery commander. Of course, I'd gone there dressed in my best service dress with my tennis things to change into there. We weren't supposed to go outside the gun area other than in uniform, and I'd made the great mistake of wearing a pair of suede shoes. Strictly speaking you shouldn't wear suede shoes with uniform, not really done, unless you're cavalry.

Barrett saw me in these shoes and gave me a real ticking off in front of the girls we were about to play tennis with. I could have crawled into a matchbox. It didn't make me like him any the more, considering I didn't like him in the first place. A bit of a *faux pas* on my part I suppose.

In 1988, my wife Peggy and I went over to Uggeshall. We'd noticed in the *East Anglian Daily Times* that they were advertising fundraising cream teas and so on in Uggeshall at the old school near our old gun position, so we drove up there. There, manning a potted plant stall, was Barbara Saunders. She had married, lived in Nigeria for years, her husband had died, and she had come back to live in the village where she'd been born and brought up fifty years earlier. She remembered Michael and me, and we spent a very pleasant hour chatting. Amazing how small the world is, really.

The quiet routine of our job on coastal defence carried on, and it really was pretty quiet. Our greatest moments of excitement came with a couple of attacks by Junkers Ju88s. They caused little to no damage so I think it was probably just the crew emptying their guns at us as they went home.

All through that summer the Battle of Britain was going on, but there wasn't so much going on over our part of East Anglia. It was mostly happening more to the south of East Anglia, south of the Thames, and over London, so we didn't see very much of it.

We felt a bit out of things. We had to tell ourselves that coastal defence was pretty vital and we were still under threat of invasion. We had a job to do and we just had to sit there and wait.

It got rather boring at times. I would find myself sitting up at the OP in the dark looking out to sea, and beginning to philosophise to myself. I remember writing to my father and saying that I realised for the first time the difference between thinking about something objectively and subjectively. I suppose I'd never given it much thought, looking at a problem dispassionately. If it's a difficult problem you have to look at it clearly and analytically. Looking at something objectively is just that, particularly when it is as deep, dark and impenetrable as the ocean at night.

SEPTEMBER 1940 – SOTTERLEY PARK

Some time in late September, Tony Ryder, who was with the left section in Sotterley Park, was swapped over with me and went to Uggeshall with Michael Harbinson. I went over to the left section at Sotterley Park, and Douglas Beaton joined us.

The owner of Sotterley Hall, Colonel Barnes, was away with the Scots Guards, and his wife and their family were living there in the attics. I suppose that was the fate of a lot of the families whose big country houses were requisitioned by the army. (image 6)

The move meant I now had two OPs to do duty with, and I also had to get to know the men in the other gun positions in Sotterley Park. We had one OP at Covehithe, just south of Lowestoft, and the other at Easton Broad.

During the autumn, before the weather got too bad, Royal Engineers 'sappers' came out to Easton Broad and made us a new OP on the cliff edge. They simply dug out a deep hole, and then built a cubic, thick-walled concrete chamber inside it. We got into that by climbing down a ladder. That was where we rested whilst we were on duty there, No.1 OP. (image 7)

When your turn came to act as look-out, you had to go for about 15 to 20 feet along an underground tunnel about 2-foot-square leading from the concrete chamber. At the end of this tunnel you had to climb another ladder that led into the actual OP itself. It was like a large cylindrical pillar box, only about 2'6" in diameter, with a visor that slid open sideways, making an opening just like a letterbox.

We then had a full view north towards Lowestoft and down to the south towards Walberswick. It was jolly cold. There was a most uncomfortable seat and footrest, and there was a separate seat, backing on to the front, where the signaller had to sit. He wore his earphones for communicating back to the battery should we have to fire the guns. Luckily we never did, at least not in anger. It was about the most uncomfortable place you can imagine. (image 8)

Later that month, they made a third OP that was along the seafront at Southwold itself, just past the lighthouse to the south. The OP was created in a holiday bungalow. The windows were bricked up, leaving just grills for visibility out to sea to both north and south.

Again, it was very cold but at least there was a kitchen where we could brew up some tea. And, believe it or not, the incredible thing was that there was a 'chippy', a proper fish and chip shop, in the street round the corner just behind this OP. A proper *Dad's Army* situation again. One of the team used to go out to buy fish and chips whilst the others were in their turn looking out to sea, watching for a German invasion.

When Christmas came, I phoned my father on Christmas Day, and when he answered he was very tired. He was the engineer responsible for all the gas street mains, and on Christmas Eve the Germans had bombed Manchester very heavily. He had spent the night trying to put out fires in the gas mains. At one time, I understand, he had to be dragged out unconscious from one of the pits he'd climbed down to shut off the gas supply by dealing with some valve or other. Very dangerous. Apparently he was recommended for a medal for that but nothing came of it.

In the early autumn of 1940, I bought a car at Mann Egerton's in Lowestoft, a Morris 16/6. The wartime ration of petrol was only 3½ gallons and I paid £12-10s for the car. Soon I found out that the front axle was bent, so I took it back and got my money back. That was my very short episode of owning a car. I didn't have another one except for occasional hired cars for holidays and special events until just before I went out to Germany in October 1961, during my second army career.

Christmas 1940 was my first Christmas with the regiment and on that day, whatever our duties, we all came together for the dinner. I think we did the meal in two sittings. The tradition of the officers serving the troops their Christmas dinner was followed. All in all it was a good day.

For the next three months of January, February and March of 1941, we carried on with routine duties. It was very cold and very damp. I seemed to live in Wellington boots. There was mud all around the guns, and there was a rather muddy walk across the park from Sotterley Hall where we were sleeping.

I must mention here my batman, Scarr, who was with me all the time I was with B Battery of 53 Heavy Regiment. He was a great chap. He'd been a pre-war 'rough rider' with horses. We didn't have any horses, but he was a very well-trained soldier in every way. Before joining the army he'd been an apprentice undertaker. He used to entertain us with gruesome stories about what happened sometimes when he was at work, but I won't go into those. He'd served in India for six years and was extremely competent. He looked after me extraordinarily well for the whole time I was with B Battery.

When I was off duty at Sotterley, I played chess with a local chap called Ralph Dyson. When he came to see Peggy and me after the war, he told us his wife had left him and their young son and gone off with an American Air Force chap later in the war. I only mention it in passing because it was something that seemed to happen pretty often towards the end. All very sad but a sign of the times.

While we were at Sotterley, we made quite a thing about mounting the guard each evening in front of the main entrance to the hall. Everyone took their turn at guard duty. It was a change from duty at the gun position and gave everyone a chance to get away from the muddy conditions by the guns and tidy themselves up for guard duty. One would have thought it would be tedious, but it was a welcome break from the monotony of life at the gun positions.

For the few officers, drivers, signallers and observation post assistant (OPA or OP Ack) who had alternate duties at the OPs and the guns, there was more variety than for the poor blokes who were stuck at the gun positions all the time. I suppose you could call that a variety of tedium for those whose duties lay entirely at the guns. It continued to be very important that they had regular time off duty to let their hair down to offset the tedium a bit.

APRIL 1941 – SHOTTISHAM

In early April we had orders for the battery to move about 35 miles further south, near to Woodbridge. This time all the four guns were going to be together in the woods near Shottisham, about 4 miles south-east of the famous Sutton Hoo Viking ship's burial site.

Our wagon lines (basically a parking lot for all the non-essential vehicles) were to be at Ipswich. The only vehicles to be at the gun position were those for collecting rations or for taking people where they needed to be, such as the OP. At this point our only OP was at Bawdsey Manor on the mouth of the River Deben, which was a likely spot for any enemy landings.

First of all we had to get the guns there and out of the very muddy conditions at Uggeshall and Sotterley. Each section of two guns went separately down to Shottisham. It took the whole day just to move those 35 miles starting pretty early in the morning. We left the guns overnight before putting them into position because it was a whole day's job to get the guns in properly. Getting that holdfast level and exactly into position was quite a tricky business.

Conditions at Shottisham on the gun site were very much better than at Uggeshall and Sotterley as far as general comfort was concerned. There was sandy subsoil, we didn't have the mud, and there was, we hoped, better weather coming.

We had several changes of officers there. Major Barrett was replaced by Major Silver, who was a much better commander and had served with heavy guns in the First World War. It was very distressing that Major Silver's eldest son, who was a first lieutenant on submarines, was lost at sea whilst we were at Shottisham.

Later Tony Ryder was replaced by my friend Douglas Beaton. Rocky Warwick was replaced by Chambers, and later on Chambers was replaced by Brian Hopkins.

Chambers was an international hockey player and, we thought, quite a good chap. Our reaction was a rather hard reflection of attitudes in wartime when he was discharged out of the army after a time under a 'trick cyclist'. The psychiatrist said he had anxiety neurosis and was, therefore, not fit for further war service. So off he went back to the civilian life, which every one of us would have preferred too. Our reaction to that, probably unfairly, was that he had no guts and we would be better off without him when the bullets were flying and our own lives might depend on him.

There were a couple of incidents in the mess at St Lawrence, very minor but we noted them at the time and referred to them often afterwards. When we were having dinner one day, having got as far as the dessert, Chambers lit a cigarette. Major Silver, the battery commander said, heavy with sarcasm: "Do you mind me eating whilst you smoke?" Chambers retired in haste and embarrassment. In the end we weren't sorry to see him go.

When Michael Harbinson left the battery and went for specialised training in counter-battery work, his replacement was Mike Morrow, who proved a very worthwhile addition to our complement of officers.

Before Michael Harbinson left us, he and I went together on a three-day course on counter-battery work at Bredfield Rectory, where 11 Corps HQ was, of which we were now part.

After we'd finished this course, which we'd found very interesting, Michael Harbinson, who was senior to me, was posted to become a specialist in counter-battery work. Later on, during the Normandy campaign, Michael went over to France and was involved in 'flash spotting', trying to pinpoint the position of enemy guns by flash and sound. When the V2 rockets were being sent over against England from bases in Holland, he was involved in the very skilled business of getting a sighting from the vapour trails. I believe we had quite a lot of success in spotting these and having their sites destroyed by the RAF.

While we were at Shottisham we were issued with Molotov cocktails. They had to be kept under water as they were made with a mixture of phosphorus. We never actually used them, but we were shown how to.

One of the saddest things that happened at Shottisham was that a chap called Driver Gilbert was very badly injured. At that time, with the fear of enemy parachutists being dropped all over the place, at night the small country roads had wires pulled across them at chest height. Most of those roads had trees lining them on both sides, and the wires could be drawn across fairly tightly from a tree on one side to one on the other. Poor old Gilbert was coming back on his motorbike from Ipswich from a duty there rather late one night and ran into one of those wires which cut his mouth right open. He managed to get back to the battery position, where he was given First Aid and went to bed. But the pain from his mouth was so bad that he shot himself. It was very, very distressing.

A couple of miles away from the gun positions at Shottisham was a fake airfield that had been put in by sappers from the Royal Engineers, with the whole construction being under the control of the RAF. There was all that one would expect on a real airfield. They had shapes of aircraft in some sort of fabric, blown up to full size to look like real planes. They had runways marked, a control tower, and lights showing at night. It was somewhere between Rendlesham Forest and the village of Sutton. Of course it was intended to draw attention away from Martlesham Airfield, which was a very active fighter station.

The fake airfield was bombed several times while we were at Shottisham but, luckily, nothing actually hit us. Lucky, too, as we hadn't bothered then to dig any slit-trenches like we certainly did later in Normandy. If we had been bombed at Shottisham, there would have been pretty severe casualties. Unless, of course, the bomb was one of the wooden bombs the Germans are said to have dropped on one of the fake airfields. I do hope that was a true story.

It was whilst we were at Shottisham in June 1941 that the Germans invaded Russia, and we used to listen to the radio every day. The news was very happily received by us because it meant there was less pressure on our own country for the time being.

In the meantime there was an organisation called the Entertainments National Service Association (ENSA), which recruited a lot of show business people and entertainers, and they came round to various services' camps. On one occasion we had a singer, whose name I can't remember, who came to entertain the battery. She came into the men's messing marquee, looking quite attractive wearing a long red dress with full sleeves, and one of the songs she sang was *Waltzing, waltzing, with you in my arms*, to great cheers from the men. As she was throwing her long arms upwards towards the end of her performance, great sweaty patches appeared. She met with great applause as she had sung very well, but after she'd gone, to our great shame, we derived much entertainment from those sweaty patches. When Douglas Beaton and I met again many years later this was one of the first things we remembered. Awful, I know. We were young.

Now the changes in the battery's officer personnel were established, I found myself to be in the position of senior subaltern. So there was a chance that in the not too distant future I might be promoted to a battery captaincy.

Whilst this was in the air, an army letter came round asking for volunteers to go for training as air OP pilots. The snag was that they were only offering 2/- (10p) a day extra. I thought a lot about it but decided the most sensible thing was to stay where I was. I suppose ambition got the better of me. No doubt it would have been very exciting to have become an air OP pilot, but it wasn't to be.

Soon after that Joe Baker, our battery captain, went off to some other job for a few months on a special attachment. While he was away I was given captain's pay until he came back, which was very useful.

DISTRACTIONS AT BAWDSEY MANOR

We only had the one OP then, and that was on the roof of Bawdsey Manor. Bawdsey Manor was a fascinating place, built in the middle of the nineteenth century. The house was very well fitted out, with oak panelling, polished floors, ornate ceilings, and so on. It was also where the first RDF (Radio Direction Finding) early radar station was sited and early experiments were carried out there, so it was a very secretive site.

The best thing for us was that Bawdsey Manor itself was used for a Women's Auxiliary Air Force (WAAF) officer cadet training unit (OCTU) so that to go to our OP on the roof we had to go through the WAAF quarters. A tricky business, passing through up the staircases unannounced. Tricky maybe, but a very popular duty. I became friendly with one of the WAAF cadets, who was called Kirsty. We met a couple of times in Woodbridge but nothing came of it. Naturally, Douglas Beaton and I monopolised that OP.

One of the more enjoyable things about the OP was that the Highland Light Infantry were stationed there, and their job was to guard the coast from Hollesley down to the entrances to Harwich near Felixstowe. They had erected scaffolding all along the beaches, creating defences that were supposed to stop enemy tanks from coming ashore and getting off the beach. (image 11)

Right in front of Bawdsey Manor, where this WAAF OCTU was, they hadn't mined the beach and they hadn't put the scaffolding up, leaving a gap so that the WAAF cadets could go and have their daily swim in the sea. Of course, when we were on the roof of the manor at our OP during the summer, and when we should have been continually looking out to sea, we were using our binoculars to focus on those girls swimming in the sea. After all, there wasn't a lot of opportunity for contact with female company when we were on coastal defence at our gun positions miles from nowhere.

SEPTEMBER 1941 – PRETEND GUNS AT ST LAWRENCE

In the late summer of 1941, we were moved again. There was still fear of invasion. We went further south to the north side of the Dengie Peninsula on the south coast of the River Blackwater. Our battery position was at St Lawrence, about a mile from the river and about 4 miles from the coast.

We had an OP at Sales Point near the site of the old Saxon church of St Peter about a mile and a half from where the Bradwell Nuclear Power Station is now. The guns had been put along the line of a hedge to the south of the old Georgian rectory, which had been requisitioned. The main messes and ablutions were in and around the rectory but, strangely, our officers' mess was in a modern bungalow about a quarter of a mile from the gun position.

There was a Finnish barque, a four-masted sailing ship, which had been impounded when the war started. We could always tell the direction of the tide on the river because the barque swung to and fro on a single anchor.

The OP was rather tricky there. The countryside was so flat it was difficult to see out to sea so we had to erect a tower from scaffolding with a sort of shaky ladder up the side. It was rather grim when you got to the top. You didn't feel remotely safe.

After we'd got established at St Lawrence, we built a miniature gunnery range in the basement of the officers' mess bungalow This was really a landscape on canvas netting. We drew a map of what the landscape was supposed to represent. We had an instructor in gunnery from 11 Corps who came along regularly, and we had a couple of hours on the miniature range. A target was pointed out on this landscape, and then each of us had a turn giving the orders to do a battery shoot. The instructor was perched below the landscape, which was set at an angle, the slope rising to the back so that the scene was as if it was mountainous country.

He set off puffs of smoke from below where the shell would have landed. He had a little artillery board to calculate this. It was all excellent practice. Happily, we did have at least some proper live practice later on when we went down to Larkhill during December 1941.

NOVEMBER 1941 – MATTERS OF THE HEART

The nearest place for the chaps to go when they had time off was Maldon. Our passion wagons used to take the men off duty in the evening into Maldon (about 12 miles away).

It was an especially happy day for me when I first saw Peggy on 7 November 1941 in Maldon, and was introduced to her on 15 November. Later on I met her again on a weekend leave from 29 to 30 November, which I spent in Maldon at the Blue Boar Hotel, and Peggy and I had dinner there together.

At the time she was working in North Fambridge for a chap called Stuart, who was a rather eccentric genius. His wife was one of the Swinburne family, of the famous poet Swinburne. Stuart had developed some innovative way of putting a thread on particularly hard steel screws and their bolts, which were needed for manufacturing armaments.

Fambridge was about 12 or 13 miles away from the battery position, so I used to cycle over in the dark to see her. In those days there were no street lights, certainly not in the country anyway. You weren't allowed to show a proper light beam in front of you and the light had to be hooded with only a very small beam, so it was a bit hairy at times.

But the truth was simple. We had more or less instantly fallen in love with each other and knew we wanted to spend the rest of our lives together. I suppose we also knew in the wartime world we were living in the rest of our lives ran the risk of not being very long. So, just under four weeks after we'd met, I asked Peggy to marry me. When you don't know if you'll still be alive in a few months' time it focuses things a bit. We were certainly not alone in doing this. (image 9)

That was on 11 December 1941, and I had a week's leave to follow, so I went off the following day and told my father that I was going to get married. I went on leave on the Friday and waited until Tuesday evening, when there was a decent opportunity to tell him what I'd planned to do.

The Brains Trust was on the radio, and I switched that off, and said: "Dad, I've got something important to tell you." And I told him I was getting married.

He sounded a bit shattered, and said: "What do you propose to do if you survive the war?"

"Go back to Cambridge and finish my degree," I said.

"Who's going to pay for that?"

"You are." I said.

"You can think again, chum." he replied, "I'm certainly not going to pay for that. You must look after yourself. Once you're married, your family is your responsibility, and you must see to your own future then. Once you're married, and you've made your own decision, you've made your own bed, you lie on it."

He continued, "However, what I will do," and this was extremely generous really, and he kept his promise, "for every £100 you save, I'll give you £100".

So Peggy and I talked this over before we married and we decided that we'd put the big sum in those days of £16-13s-6d into the bank each month, and that would make £200 a year. We kept that up until I left the army after the war, and with the money that my father gave us, we had enough to begin to buy our house when I eventually went back to Cambridge.

JANUARY 1942 – LARKHILL, SALISBURY PLAIN

In early in January 1942, after Christmas when, as tradition dictated, we served the men their Christmas dinner, we went down to Larkhill practice camp to shoot guns in actuality rather than just on the miniature range. It was a terribly cold journey down to Salisbury Plain. I drove down in an open Leyland cab. Those lorries just had canvas doors, no hood, bitterly cold, I don't think I'd ever felt so frozen.

JANUARY 1942 – MARRIAGE AT MALDON

After the practice camp, when I came back we had to complete the final arrangements for our wedding – reading of Banns, and booking things in Cambridge for our honeymoon, our reception, and so forth.

We were married on Thursday, 29 January 1942. My father and stepmother came down from Altrincham in Cheshire. I'd booked them in at the Blue Boar Hotel in Maldon after getting them a permit to enter what was then a restricted zone, being so near the east coast, and my father met Peggy for the first time the evening before we married. We were married at All Saints' Church, Maldon, at a quarter past nine in the morning. We had a very brief Reception with just a few of our friends at the Blue Boar Hotel, almost next door to the church, and caught the 11.15 a.m. train to Cambridge for our honeymoon. We had forty-eight hours leave at the University Arms Hotel in Cambridge. (image 10)

In all the excitement I left a very valuable thing on the train: my sword-stick, which my batman, Scarr, had given me. It was about 18 inches long with a rather nice leather handle and a short sword fitted into it within a leather scabbard. Naturally, we never saw that again.

The railway line went through Witham to Braintree and then on to Bishops Stortford and via Shelford to Cambridge. Sadly the very pretty line was closed under the 'Beeching Axe' after the war. On our honeymoon, we had pretty mixed weather – fog, rain, snow, everything you think of as January.

We came back by the same route as far as Maldon on the Saturday a couple of days later. We caught a bus to Tillingham, where we'd arranged to have rooms there belonging to a Mrs Chell, where I could go when off duty. Again it was a very snowy day and, whilst going to Tillingham on the bus, we had to get out and help to push the bus up a particularly steep hill to keep it moving. This was near a place appropriately called Steeple, and was all rather tricky.

When I was able to have twenty-four hours off duty with meals there at Tillingham, my rations were actually brought round by a chap called Driver Vickerson. Funnily enough, some years after the war when I had rejoined the army in 1950, I was sent out to the Korean War and went down to Southampton to get on board the troopship. One of the first people I saw on board the ship was Driver Vickerson, who'd been recalled from the reserve and was himself back in the gunners going off to Korea. I took that as a lucky omen in 1950 when we set off but that's another story.

Just one silly thing about our rooms in Tillingham. We had a sitting room to ourselves and, of course, a bedroom. One morning when getting out of bed, my foot went right through the floor. It must have been pretty rotten but Mrs Chell got very snotty about it and wrote a vicious letter to my battery commander, saying I'd deliberately damaged her floor. Needless to say, nobody bought that.

There was one slightly embarrassing incident after we had come back from our honeymoon on the Saturday evening. My battery commander Major Silver had said before our wedding: "Don't worry about getting back to the battery position, you go back to Tillingham and come and have tea with us in the mess. Bring your new wife along on Sunday afternoon."

So that was the very thing we did, of course. When I went to open the mess door there was Major Silver waiting for us, and he said: "Ah hello, Mainwaring, I'd given you up – I thought you were never going to come back."

Of course he was joking, but it was highly embarrassing for poor old Peggy on the first time she'd been to our officers' mess, with all the officers assembled to greet her. We had a lovely afternoon, actually, but Peggy was terribly worried thinking I'd committed a grievous sin in coming back late, even though Major Silver was only winding me up. So that was the end of our honeymoon, and a return to duty.

MARCH 1942 – HUNWORTH, NORFOLK COAST

Meanwhile life continued at St Lawrence. As far as Peggy and I were concerned it was a blissful six weeks before a new bombshell to us as newlyweds came. The battery was told it was to move to Holt in Norfolk at pretty short notice.

We had to give up our rooms at Tillingham and pay a month's rent in lieu of notice. Peggy went back to the Black Cottage at Langford, for the duration as it turned out, and I had to take my part in getting the guns dismantled and out of action.

It was a very cold mid-March. When we moved I was able to let Peggy know when we would be on our way. She went to Maldon and waved sadly as we drove past in the High Street on our way to Holt. Communication then was rather difficult. The Black Cottage was a mile from any phone, and 3 miles from the nearest shop, and very remote. So we had to arrange by letter to speak on the telephone.

Peggy:
There were often air-raids at night. We had the air-raid warning siren on the waterworks over the way with its wailing noise, it was so near us, a terrific row, you couldn't sleep through it. Then you'd hear that awful noise of the German planes, a throbbing droning sound…you knew they were German. You sat there wondering if you were going to be 'target for tonight'.

The move to Holt took two full days. When we got there we had to pull the guns on their trailers under the trees round the heavily tree-lined streets near Greshams School. The officers and men were billeted

Harry Mainwaring Snr in 1912, before the outbreak of the First World War in 1914 (Jes Mainwaring)

2. *Uncle Jacques, Royal Flying Corps, with his RE8 biplane, March 1918 (Jes Mainwaring)*

3. *Harry aged 20 in 1940 (Jes Mainwaring)*

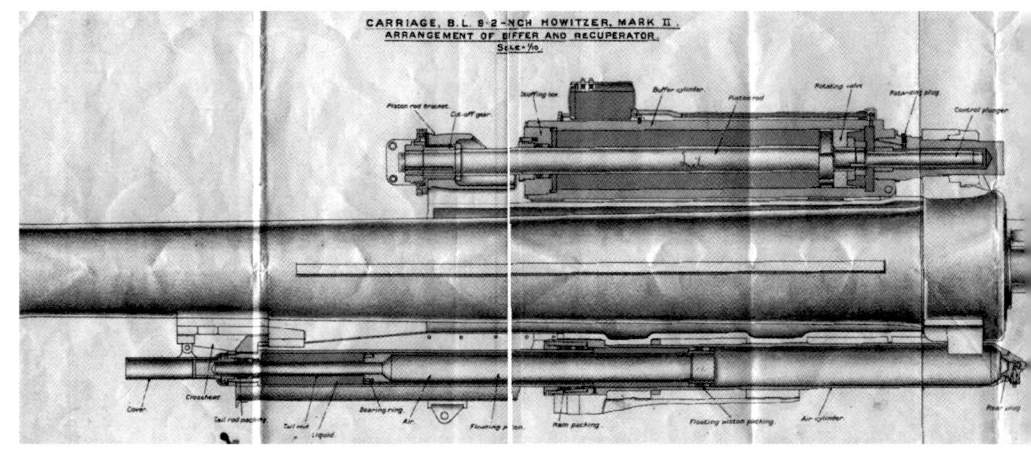

4. *Section detail drawing of 9.2" howitzer Mk II*

5. *Line of howitzers at practice camp, Larkhill*

6. *Sotterly Hall*

7. *Harry's wartime OS map, marked up with his east coast OPs (Jes Mainwaring)*

8. *The tide of time. No. 1 OP showing the effect of eighty years of erosion of the soft cliffs (Simon Mainwaring)*

9. *Peggy in 1942 (Jes Mainwaring)*

10. *Harry; and Peggy Mainwaring, just married. January; 1942 (Jes Mainwaring)*

11. *Tank traps on the estuary of the River Deben beside Bawdsey Manor (Jes Mainwaring)*

12. *Royal Artillery 155mm 'Long Tom' advancing in Normandy, 1944*

13. *American 155mm 'Long Tom' on static display (Mark Pellegrini)*

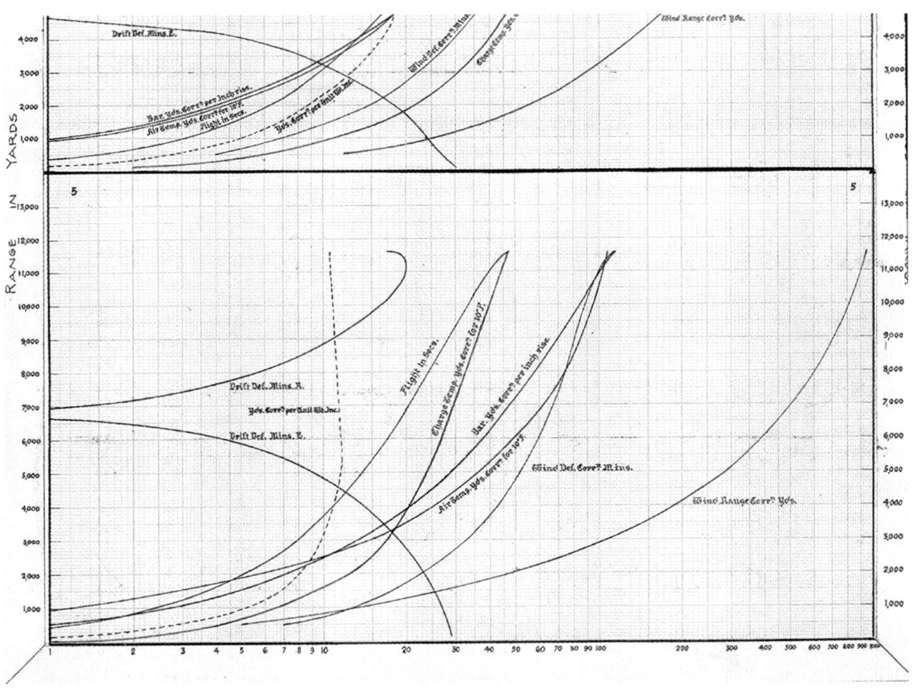

14. *Logs RA meteor telegram 9.2" howitzer range tables, Charge 5 designed by Harry Mainwaring Snr (Jes Mainwaring)*

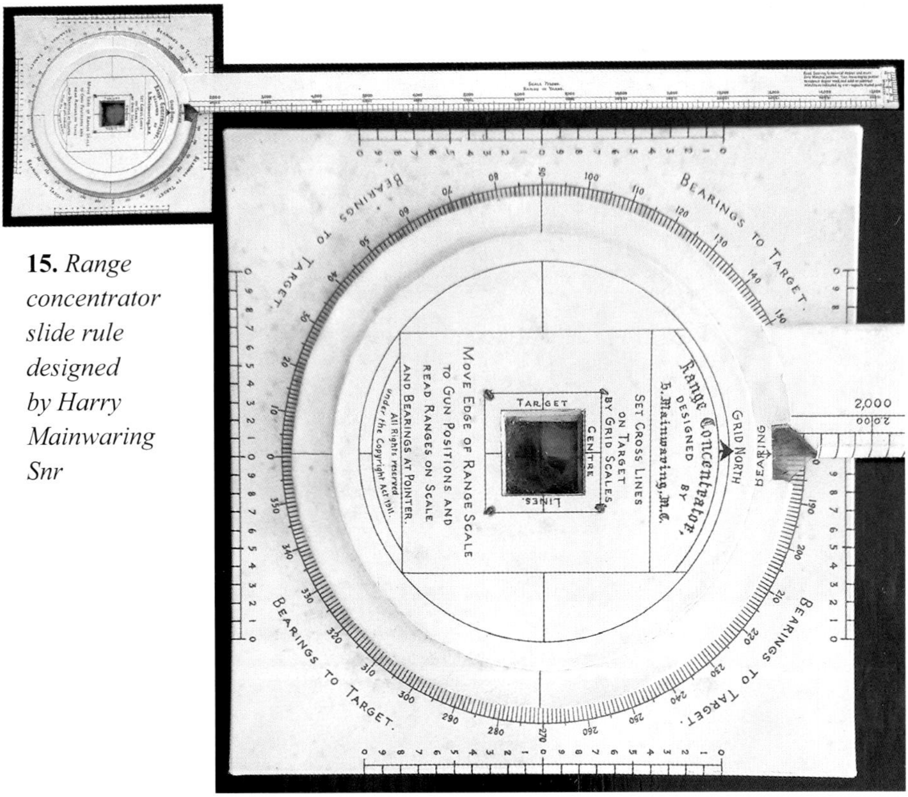

15. *Range concentrator slide rule designed by Harry Mainwaring Snr*

Range concentrator target information display (Jes Mainwaring)

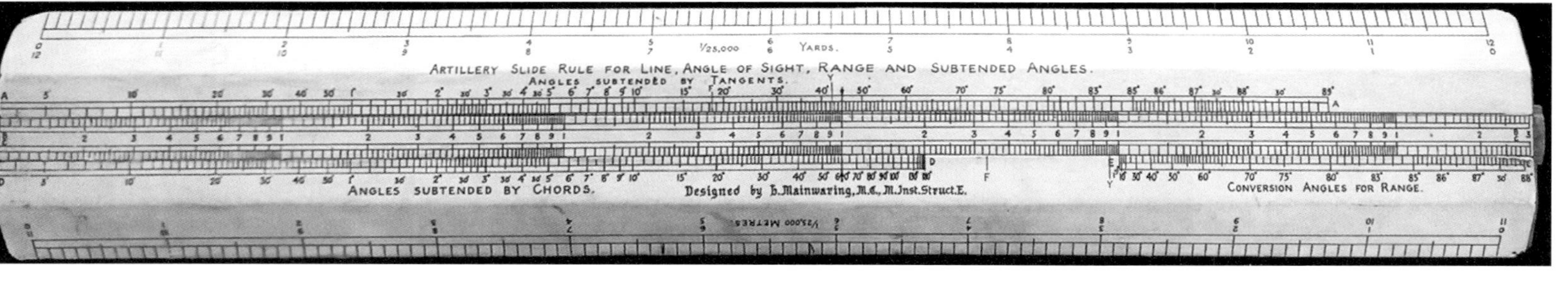

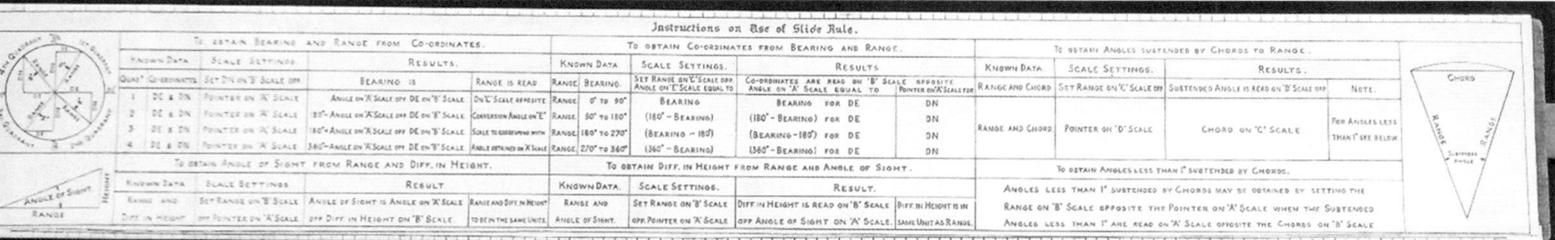

Instructions on Use of Slide Rule.

To obtain Bearing and Range from Co-ordinates.

Quad.ᵗ	Known Data — Co-ordinates	Scale Settings — Set DN on 'B' Scale opp.	Results — Bearing is	Range is read
1	DE & DN	Pointer on 'A' Scale	Angle on 'A' Scale off DE on 'B' Scale	On 'C' Scale opposite
2	DE & DN	Pointer on 'A' Scale	180°−Angle on 'A' Scale off DE on 'B' Scale	Conversion Angle on 'E'
3	DE & DN	Pointer on 'A' Scale	180°+Angle on 'A' Scale off DE on 'B' Scale	Scale to correspond with
4	DE & DN	Pointer on 'A' Scale	360°−Angle on 'A' Scale off DE on 'B' Scale	Angle obtained on 'X' Scale

To obtain Co-ordinates from Bearing and Range.

Known Data — Range	Bearing	Scale Settings — Set Range on 'C' Scale opp. Angle on 'E' Scale equal to	Results — Co-ordinates are read on 'B' Scale opposite Angle on 'A' Scale equal to	Pointer on 'A' Scale for
Range	0° to 90°	Bearing	Bearing for DE	DN
Range	90° to 180°	(180°−Bearing)	(180°−Bearing) for DE	DN
Range	180° to 270°	(Bearing−180°)	(Bearing−180°) for DE	DN
Range	270° to 360°	(360°−Bearing)	[360°−Bearing] for DE	DN

To obtain Angles subtended by Chords to Range.

Known Data	Scale Settings	Results	Note
Range and Chord	Set Range on 'C' Scale opp.	Subtended Angle is read on 'D' Scale opp.	For Angles less than 1° see below
Range and Chord	Pointer on 'D' Scale	Chord on 'C' Scale	

To obtain Angle of Sight from Range and Diff. in Height.

Known Data	Scale Settings	Result	
Range and Diff. in Height	Set Range on 'B' Scale off Pointer on 'A' Scale	Angle of Sight is Angle on 'A' Scale off Diff. in Height on 'B' Scale	Range and Diff. in Height to be in the same units

To obtain Diff. in Height from Range and Angle of Sight.

Known Data	Scale Settings	Result	
Range and Angle of Sight.	Set Range on 'B' Scale opp. Pointer on 'A' Scale	Diff. in Height is read on 'B' Scale off Angle of Sight on 'A' Scale.	Diff. in Height is in same Unit as Range.

To obtain Angles less than 1° subtended by Chords.

Angles less than 1° subtended by Chords may be obtained by setting the Range on 'B' Scale opposite the Pointer on 'A' Scale when the Subtended Angles less than 1° are read on 'A' Scale opposite the Chords on 'B' Scale.

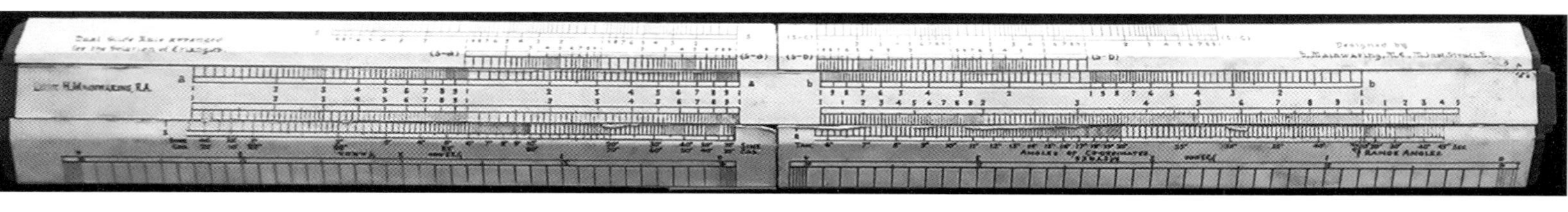

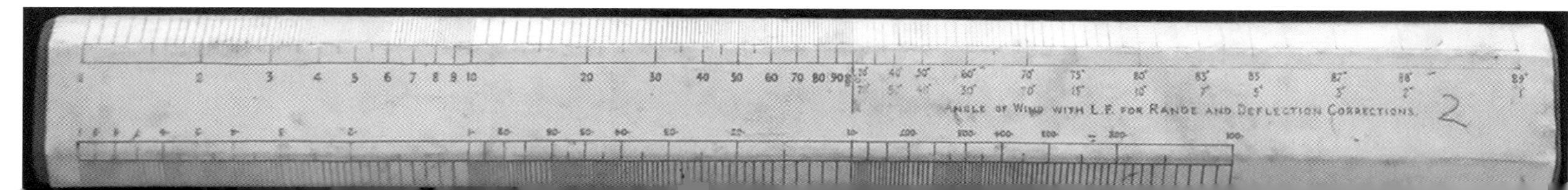

16. *Artillery slide rules designed by Harry Mainwaring Snr (Jes Mainwaring)*

in various buildings at the school, I was in one of the housemasters' houses.

Whilst we were parked there we had to go and reconnoitre the positions for the guns at Hunworth, a village about 2 miles south of Holt. A path ran slightly downhill towards a stream in the extensive grounds of the rectory and this gave a decent field of fire when we had cleared the trees and shrubs away. The guns would be firing out to sea over the Norfolk coast, to the east and west of Weybourne. All in all it took us a bit of time to move the guns into their new positions.

We had the command post and the cookhouse in the rectory garden. I don't think the rector liked any of it very much, but still it had to be done.

Whilst we were at Hunworth we had our first experience of a NAAFI van coming very occasionally with goodies, chocolates, etc., and that sort of thing. The officers' mess was in the doctor's house, just across the stream from the guns. A very pleasant situation as far as we were concerned.

We had three OPs, one on Blakeney Church, one on Cley Church, and the other on the steeply sloping hillside just above the Weybourne anti-aircraft practice camp, which had become established there by then.

As usual we had to lay all the signal lines from the guns up to the OPs and reconnoitre the route just behind Holt itself. It was quite tricky having to put the wires across the road high enough to miss the traffic. At that time it was all restricted area around the east coast, so there was very little traffic. But there were plenty of high-sided army vehicles if not much else.

Of local interest to me was that the old ruined Weybourne Priory was founded by Sir Ralph Mainwaring, Justiciary of Chester, in the twelfth century. At that time the Mainwaring family had land in Norfolk and in Cheshire. William the Conqueror had split up the lands he gave his followers in various parts of the country to keep them from getting too powerful in any one place.

However, in the gun position at Hunworth, Douglas Beaton proved himself to be very keen and particularly adept at camouflage. He was quite an artistic chap and I should think our guns were amongst the best camouflaged along the east coast.

We were completely static, and had to concrete the guns in. Then, even though we were in a static position, we started a series of mobile exercises, so it became clear we would not be there for long. We didn't quite know what was to follow, but the 59th (Newfoundland) Heavy Regiment came and took over our static positions when we went later for mobile training with new guns, 7.2" howitzers.

LIFE GOES ON AT HUNWORTH

Peggy came to stay at Hunworth Rectory for Whitsun weekend. It was very pleasant having her there for a break although one dreadfully embarrassing thing happened.

Peggy and I went to the rectory at the invitation of the rector for supper with him and his wife. He was a very short-tempered man. It seems he and his wife had quarrelled and he picked up the joint of meat, a very small joint too in those days of rationing, and threw it at his wife. That really shocked us as we were very calm and peaceful people, and there was this chap absolutely raving at his poor wife. Very awkward and very difficult.

On another occasion at Hunworth, Peggy came up and stayed for a night in a house that John Stone and Bernard Elkins had rented for their wives within reach of their batteries. John and Bernard had both joined the regiment with me in March 1940. John had been posted to A Battery, Bernard to C Battery, me to B Battery. Another great friend of ours, Bill Huntingdon, had gone to D Battery. Bill had been married in the late summer of 1941 and I had been his best man, so I'd managed to get a forty-eight-hour leave and went up to his wedding at Solihull. Later on in the war the four of us all became battery commanders as majors.

Following the move to Holt with the other batteries also moving to the same area, regimental HQ (RHQ) moved up to Keswick Hall, near Norwich.

JULY 1942 – SIX MONTHS AT RHQ

After some time at Hunworth I was posted to RHQ in Keswick Hall as assistant adjutant, which was a great surprise. This started a six months' interlude at RHQ, first as assistant adjutant and later as adjutant.

Later, when I finally retired from the army in 1967 and was deputy secretary of the Cambridge University Institute of Education, Keswick Hall had become a teacher training college for which the institute was responsible, so I still had a connection with it long after the war.

However, the cream of jobs in the gunners is with a battery, with the guns or at the OP. So although I was glad to have the experience as adjutant at Keswick Hall, I was far happier when the time came finally to go back to a battery.

Meanwhile, elsewhere the war was making some progress. On 20 August, which was also my birthday, the Dieppe Raid took place under pressure for a second front. Very sadly a lot of Canadians were killed, but it was an action that provided valuable experience and made a huge contribution towards planning for the D-Day operations nearly two years later.

Later in the summer Peggy came up to Norwich once or twice from Saturday to Sunday so we stayed at the Maid's Head Hotel in Norwich whilst she was there.

Peggy:

I was walking one particular day, it was a very hot day, passing by some houses and suddenly...these dogfights used to appear suddenly...there were fighter planes flying around with guns firing and spent bullets raining down and clattering on the roofs. Someone called out "Come in here", so in I went. On that occasion I think they said we shot down five planes.

There was one particular bomber they shot down, I think they must have hit the crew. The plane was out of control and coming down in a spiral, going in a bigger and bigger spiral and getting lower and lower. I remember thinking, I hope it doesn't come down here. When it was coming over you couldn't tell, it just went lower and lower. Of course, what looks very near is often not as close as it seems. We didn't know where it eventually went down at the time, but it was actually in the Maypole Road near Heybridge, very close to a farmhouse. There weren't a lot of buildings close to where it crashed, just this farmhouse, but it didn't do any damage. All these crewmen were ripped to ribbons, pieces of them were hanging up in the trees, the ARP [air-raid precautions] men with their bags were picking up bits with a spike.

In September, John Stone, who was the previous adjutant, having gone earlier into RHQ from A Battery, was promoted to major and went to command my old B Battery. Major Silver had been posted away as a lieutenant colonel, and I was then promoted to captain and adjutant, which was certainly useful administrative experience. From Keswick Hall as adjutant I had the job of moving RHQ up to Sheringham.

Peggy came up for several weekends there from Langford by train from Witham, when we stayed at the Dormy House Hotel. The officers' mess was up a *cul-de-sac* near the golf course, a very quiet sort of place. While we were there our survey officer was Tom Plewman, and John Wellman was the assistant adjutant.

A SPECIAL REMEMBRANCE

Tom Plewman's petite and vivacious wife Eliane was a fluent linguist in French, Italian and Spanish and very beautiful. She had joined the First Aid Nursing Yeomanry (FANY), those incredibly brave special operations executive (SOE) girls who were parachuted into France as secret agents.

Eliane was sent into France with her brother. As a member of the underground 'Monk' resistance circuit, she conducted a number of highly successful sabotage missions, and after some time they were brutally betrayed when they were sabotaging a railway bridge. She was captured by the Gestapo, tortured and sent to Ravensbruck, ultimately to be murdered. All that Tom was told from month to month was that she was still okay as far as they knew. Later the only news he had was that she'd been captured.

The following was more recently revealed by one of the SS guards who escorted Eliane and three other female agents, Noor Inayat Khan, Yolande Beekman and Madeleine Damerment, by train from Ravensbruck to Dachau in September 1944.

Between 08.00 a.m. and 10.00 a.m. in Dachau on 13 September, Eliane and Noor Inayat Khan held hands as they were made to kneel facing an execution mound. All four were murdered with a single shot each to the back of the neck by the Gestapo.

Eliane Plewman

Eliane's name is now on memorials at Dachau, Brookwood Memorial in Surrey, and the F Section Memorial in Valençay, France. She was only 26 years old. I will always find it terribly upsetting and sad. We were all very fond of her.

Using words used at Remembrance Sunday services by the Royal British Legion, especially thinking of Eliane Plewman and those other brave FANY girls who were murdered by the Nazis during the war:

They shall grow not old, as we that are left grow old.
Age shall not weary them nor the years condemn.
At the going down of the sun and in the morning, we will
remember them.

OCTOBER 1942 ONWARDS – THE 'AGRA' SHOOT

The major event as far as Peggy and I were concerned was that just before Christmas Peggy gave me the news that she was pregnant. Of course, that pregnancy became our first son Simon in July 1943, so from then on we were becoming a family of more than just Peggy and me.

In the larger army world, we had become army troops, part of the 8th Corps. Attached to the 8th Corps was a gunner body called the 8th AGRA (Army Group, Royal Artillery), and its function was to put down heavy fire wherever required.

The training we had to do for this had been developed just before El Alamein in October 1942, where it had been shown to be very effective. The training came over to us very quickly as part of the 8th AGRA, which consisted of ourselves as one heavy regiment with sixteen guns. There was one field regiment – 25th Field with twenty-four guns – and there were three medium regiments: 61st Medium, 63rd Medium, and 77th Medium, and they had twenty-four guns each. So the whole AGRA with five gunner regiments had 112 guns.

The training we had to do was to be able to put down what was called an 'AGRA Shoot'. That's the fire of 112 guns, controlled by one officer from his OP through his own regimental net.

When you are doing a shoot through your battery net, this simply means a group of radio sets on the same frequency, typically at a battery position and at the battery's OP.

At the battery end if, for example, you were doing a regimental shoot, the gun position officer (GPO) would have a second radio set on the regimental net and he would pass on your fire orders, which in this case would mean concentrating the fire of sixteen guns.

From your OP you would order 'regimental target' and your GPO would then pass on those orders to RHQ on their net, and at RHQ the adjutant would be in charge. He would actually be working the set and he would pass on the fire orders over the regimental net to the other batteries of the regiment. So that was the regimental net.

When you did an AGRA shoot using the AGRA net, the adjutant also had a second radio. He would have an assistant, probably the assistant adjutant, working the second radio, which was also on the AGRA net. He would pass on the orders to the AGRA and the relevant officer at the AGRA would pass on the orders to all the regiments within the AGRA, other than the originating regiment.

Using this sequence, up from the battery net via the regimental net and finally through the AGRA net, and through that to the other regiments' nets on to their individual battery nets, you would have the concentrated fire, in our case of 112 guns, which was pretty incredible.

I did several AGRA shoots in Normandy. You can make a real mess of a concentration of tanks, which I actually managed to do.

The commanding officer of our RHQ was Lieutenant Colonel Roderick MacLeod, a very fine chap. Sadly he'd been captured in the First World War at Le Cateau on 26 August 1914, so he'd only just got into that war when he was taken prisoner, and he remained a prisoner-of-war throughout that war. He became an interpreter in German. Freddy Hewitt was our second-in-command and, at the time I was the adjutant. The assistant adjutant was John Wellman, who took over from me later as adjutant. Tom Plewman was our survey officer.

When the RHQ was at Sheringham, we did an exercise called Exercise Guist. Guist is a little village a few miles south of Holt, probably about 20 miles from Sheringham. This was really a 'signal control' exercise and we had all our radios out. This was the first exercise where we'd had to do a simulated AGRA shoot controlling the fire of the whole AGRA's guns.

It was really rather amusing. We'd got a new fire-breathing brigadier, Archie Campbell, who'd won a Distinguished Service

Order (DSO) and a MC and Bar in the First World War. A very fine chap indeed. And in the middle of the night I was given an AGRA shoot to do. In theory we had the fire orders coming down from one of our batteries to me as adjutant controlling the regimental fire of the whole regiment. I then had to see that the orders were passed on to the other regiments. Without warning, Archie Campbell suddenly appeared at the door of our wagon where we'd set up our radios.

"Right, Mainwaring," said Campbell, "your assistant adjutant's just been killed by a shell splinter. You'd better just carry on with the shoot on your own."

So there I was, feeling like a fish out of water, with two head-set earphones as we had two radios working, with one earpiece on one ear and one from the second set on the other ear. I had to organise myself so that I knew what I was doing: getting the fire orders from the battery, which was on the regimental net, then passing them down on that same regimental frequency to our own other batteries. Next, I had to get on the AGRA net to the AGRA HQ, who would in turn send them on down to the other regiments of the AGRA. And they would pass them on to their own batteries.

It was the first time we'd ever done it and it was seemingly an impossible thing to do. Heaven knows how, but somehow we managed it. A couple of hours later Archie Campbell came over to our RHQ wagon, having been round to the other regiments, who were all fairly close for this signal exercise, and said: "Well, Mainwaring, I'd say you've done pretty well for a first time effort on your own." So I felt appropriately chuffed about that.

JANUARY 1943 – THE REGIMENT DIVIDES

Time passed, and with January 1943 the plan was to expand the army like mad as more recruits were coming in, more people were being called up. Planning intensively for the second front, having learnt from the experience of the Dieppe Raid, was well in hand.

As far as our 53rd Heavy Regiment was concerned we were going to be split in half. Half of the regiment was to go to Cromer to form the 56th Medium & Heavy Training Regiment, and each of the two batteries that were left were to be split in half to give the regiment its proper complement of four batteries.

The regiment was now to follow the Royal Artillery's normal practice of batteries being numbered. A and D Batteries had left, and B and C Batteries were divided into two new batteries each: 8 and 25, and 9 and 24 Heavy Batteries respectively.

The commanding officer, Roderick MacLeod, asked me to take over the new 25 Battery and Bernard Elkins to command the new 24 Battery. Bernard and I knew all the chaps who were coming to us from the former C and B Batteries as we had been with them since early 1940. Bernard, who was older than me, joined the regiment with me in March 1940, so we knew each other very well, and we knew and trusted the senior non-commissioned officers (NCOs) who were staying with us very well too.

In the Royal Artillery there are two grades of sergeant. There is a full sergeant, who wears the shape of a gun on his sleeve above his sergeant's three stripes, and there is a lance sergeant who has just the three stripes of a sergeant on his sleeve but without the gun. Both are members of the sergeants' mess, although the full sergeant has seniority and is called the No. 1 on the gun. He commands the gun detachment. and is completely responsible for the gun.

When Bernard and I formed our two new batteries, 24 & 25 Heavy Batteries, each had two full sergeants from our former batteries and two lance sergeants, who were then promoted to full sergeant. That gave us each four No. 1's in command of our four guns. I was very lucky to get a pre-war regular, Sergeant Major Cook, as my battery sergeant major, who was absolutely first-class.

The remainder of the battery, because it was then only half strength, was made up partly from intakes of national servicemen with a few of the July 1939 Militia, who were of course very well trained. The other men were intakes of people who had been called up in the normal way during the course of the war, and they were virtually straight from their basic training.

Then, of course, we had the job of training them further on top of everything else. Those first three weeks were very busy. We had to establish the battery: get the gun detachments together, choose people for the signal section, get the drivers and men for the Light Aid Detachment (LAD) and train them. We had to organise the command post for control of the guns, and we had to decide who were to be the OPAs. It was pretty tough going, but it was quite thrilling, quite exciting.

In the weeks that followed, a more senior officer, Laurie Wass, was posted in to command 25 Battery with me as battery captain and second-in-command. I was only 23 years old at the time so it was fair enough. Happily, he was a very good chap and we got on very well together.

Very shortly after, we took delivery of our new mobile guns, which were 7.2" howitzers. We had already handed over our concreted-in guns, 9.2" howitzers from the First World War, to the 59th (Newfoundland) Heavy Regiment way back at Hunworth, so as far as we were concerned we were getting brand-new guns.

They were massive. Huge wheels with balloon tyres and when the guns were fired there was, of course, the very powerful reverse force from the exploding charge. This discharged the shell, pushing the gun itself backwards, as it was not held down by a 'trail' in the way lighter guns were with their 'split trail'. To cope with this, each gun had a very large heavy 'scotch', a wedge with its upper surface curved out through almost 90 degrees and about 4 feet high, placed against the back of the wheels, with a smaller one put against the front of the wheel. When the gun was fired it ran back up the rear scotch and then forwards up the front scotch, finally coming to rest between them. The gun-towing tractor had to be kept pretty near to the gun in order to winch the gun round to its correct line of fire if it had gone off line in running back. It was all a very tricky business when in action.

Then we got excellent news: 24 Battery and 8 Battery were keeping their 7.2″ howitzers, but 9 Battery and my own 25 Battery were going to be equipped with the American 'Long Tom' 155mm gun instead of the 7.2″ howitzers. The Long Tom had a terrific range of 27,000 yards, about 17 miles. (image 13)

The first thing then was that someone had to learn all about the 155mm gun and its equipment. This meant practice shoots with them on their artillery range, and to see their gun drill when in action. I was given the job and sent off to Bude in Cornwall to the US (Virginian) 123rd Artillery Battalion, as the American artillery call their regiments.

MY FATHER AND THE LOGARITHMS

This is an appropriate point to say something here about my father's contribution to the war effort. He was a structural and services engineer, a brilliant mathematician, and a member of the Institute of Structural Engineers, with the kind of mind that seemed to be able to think in logarithms. Whenever he encountered a recurring problem dealing with a known set of variable parameters, he would design and hand-build a fully functioning slide rule to provide rapid design solutions to the matter in hand. He too had been an artillery officer in the First World War, and understood ballistics.

Coastal defence might sound as if it was a boring slow business with nothing happening. In many respects it was. However, for twenty-four hours every day one particular mathematical job had to be done methodically and constantly, without fail.

Whenever a gun is aimed and fired you have to take into account the air pressure from the barometer and the wind speed and direction. We had little booklets, called *Range Tables*, which were used to work out how much allowance we had to make for the climatic conditions. Every four hours we were sent a meteor telegram from HQ. That gave the wind speed, the wind direction and the barometric pressure at various heights above sea level. It used to take a minimum of forty minutes, repeated every four hours, to work out the corrections needed for the entire range that our guns might have to fire in case of invasion. (image 14)

I wrote to my father and explained the problem, pointing out the delay and time being wasted before the guns could be used effectively. Also, we didn't have any brilliant mathematicians amongst the gun position assistants (GP Acks) who had to do the job, and whose work also had to be checked for any errors.

"Leave it with me and I'll think about it," he replied.

A short time later he wrote to me to say that he could resolve the problem in such a way that we could do all the work in about five minutes, but that he would need a copy of the *Range Tables*. He was afraid these would be restricted and not allowed to civilians, so I got on to the CO, Colonel Roderick MacLeod. He knew my father had been in the Royal Garrison Artillery and awarded the MC in the First World War, so he said I could send him a copy of the *Range Tables* under registered post.

We had a spare copy so I sent it to my father. He worked on them and I suppose it took about three weeks before he sent me back some wonderful charts, which are still in my possession. They consisted of logarithmic scales dealing with each charge used for the varying ranges and, in addition, a special slide rule he had prepared to go with the scales. We could then very simply and quickly work out the corrections needed for the atmospheric conditions for the various ranges at which the guns might have to fire.

My father also went on to develop another similar device, a later working version of which I also still have. Very simply, it had a central square section he originally made out of card, with a cross-wire across a piece of mica (more commonly referred to as Perspex today) in the centre, and a range arm sufficient to cover a range of 17,000 yards.

You merely turned this arm around its central pivot and it gave you the angle and range to the target from your guns at whatever map reference the target was from your gun position. It was very simple, all done in a matter of seconds instead of having to do all sorts of calculations. (image 15)

Very simply, our guns were howitzers, which are guns that can elevate the barrel, the 'piece', high up from the horizontal. The higher it is raised the further the shell will go depending on the amount of cordite in the charge that sends it off.

It was a great relief to us, and happily proved to be a great relief to gunners all over the fighting areas later on in the war. My father gave these marvellous charts and slide rules he had to the Department of Scientific Research. Development of his work continued and later in the war was used for other guns by the whole Royal Regiment of Artillery.

We had charges 1 to 5 with one bag of cordite extra per charge. When shooting at maximum range, we used five bags of cordite. We then had these five logarithmic charts, or scales, with overlaid graph lines that my father had prepared for us to use in resolving the meteor telegram. Now it was a piece of cake. Five minutes and the whole telegram was worked out. (image 16)

So my father, also Harry Mainwaring, really did a wonderful job, quite unseen in the background, to help the war effort. He never asked for any financial reward, although I believe he did maintain the copyright.

FEBRUARY 1943 – THE YANKS ARE COMING

THE US 123rd BATTALION – BUDE, CORNWALL

Going back to the American 155mm Long Tom guns and their equipment, we had to learn how the American system of controlling the fire of the guns to the target was organised.

Very simply, their system was that they ranged on what was called the 'line OT'. You had a straight line on your map from the OP to the target and you tried to range the guns by observing the shells when they landed. You had a shell bursting between you and the target, and then you had to fiddle about with more shells until you landed a shell beyond the target and your line of sight to it. You then tried to get the guns to narrow the bracket along that line OT before and beyond the target until you finally landed a shell on the target. Very expensive in ammunition, but of course the Americans were very rich and had plenty of ammunition. Far more than we ever did.

It didn't really need anyone to be very skilled at the OP to do this. You simply went on and on correcting the mistakes, however many there were.

In the Royal Artillery, however, we were taught to read the map properly, to gauge the lie of the land, and visualise where the line of fire ran along the ground from the guns to the target, where the shells would actually go. We then bracketed the shells so that they landed not between us and the target but between the guns and the target, and our bracket was one short of the target and one beyond the target. That was very much more economic.

On the range near Bude, when it came my turn to control the fire of their American guns and I was asked if I'd like to have a crack at it, I said: "I certainly would, but may I use the British system? Can I give the instructions to your guns according to the Royal Artillery way of giving the corrections? Then they'd be bracketed using the technique we've been taught to control the fire."

So I did just that. The previous American officer, a major, had done his ranging on the line OT and taken twenty-four shells to get on to the target. By this time I'd been watching their shooting closely and I'd got the lie of the land fairly well in my mind. Believe it or not I got on to the target with four shells, one slightly to the right of it. I corrected it to the left and beyond it, and then I got one short and the next hit the target. Four against twenty-four was definitely more economic and a lot quicker.

The Americans looked rather surprised, having pretty much rated us as a dead loss after Dunkirk. And they were somewhat surprised to find a British officer, a captain and not even a major, could hit the target with one sixth of the number of shells they'd used. I definitely felt 'one-up to the Royal Artillery, mate'.

HUNSTANTON

It must have been towards the end of February 1943 when I came back from this attachment to the Americans at Bude, that my battery, 25 Heavy Battery, moved to Hunstanton on the north Norfolk coast. The RHQ was in the now-demolished Station Hotel, which had been requisitioned by the army. The old railway branch line from Kings Lynn was still there, terminating at Hunstanton.

Whilst we were there Peggy came and stayed for a while in rooms overlooking the sea front not far from the battery area. She stayed with a couple of old ladies whom we called Mem and Blanche.

We still had our 7.2" howitzers at that time, and our daily routine was to do gun drill on the old Hunstanton fairground. It was strangely incongruous doing gun drill alongside the ghost train. It caused pretty loud echoes and we gave the orders very loudly too.

Then came the swap-over when we took down our 7.2" howitzers and took delivery of our new American 155mm Long Toms. The 7.2s could, of course, be moved much more swiftly down to Colchester behind our Scammell tractors at just over 20mph, rather than the 4mph with the original First World War 9.2" howitzers.

Having done the attachment with the Americans at Bude and acquired a bit of experience, I was supposed to be the expert. I was far from, but at least I had a less vague idea than anybody else in the regiment. So that earned me the job of checking all the spares and the stores.

Then we had to learn the revised gun drill. It was very much more easy for our ammunition numbers, because over the months changing from 9.2" howitzers to 7.2" howitzers, and now finally to the 155mm, the shells had gone down in weight from 290lb to 200lb, and now down to only 100lb.

Regarding the old 9.2" howitzers we'd had at Uggeshall and Shottisham, their shells weighed 290lb (about 130kg), and loading and firing the 9.2s was a much more complicated business. The 9.2" howitzer needed a loading platform, which was built on to the cradle of the gun, and had a ratchet-controlled loading device, which had to be worked by two men.

They had to raise the shell up to the breech. The shell had to be carried by the men up to the platform from the pile of ammunition stored behind the gun, a hell of a weight to carry really. And then four chaps on the platform held the 'rammer', a long 3"-diameter pole with a wide pad at the end, which was pushed against the base of the shell into the chamber beyond the breech, and then into the gun barrel. Any similarity with the old-fashioned bronze cannons used at Waterloo is purely coincidental.

That's where the copper driving bands, which were of course of softer metal, were then scored by the specially-hardened steel rifling, and that then twisted the shell on its way down the barrel as it was fired.

Behind the base of the shell after it had been rammed home, the necessary bags of cordite were placed in the chamber space and the breech was closed and twisted round so that its threads were caught against the threads of the breech block. And that meant that the breech was safely and firmly closed before the gun was fired.

With the 9.2" howitzer , the gun was actually fired by pulling a lanyard that was attached to the firing pin in the breech. It all sounds very complicated but it was very simple really. Pulling the lanyard released a very strong spring at the back of the interior of the breech block and as it sprang forward it struck the rear centre of a cartridge, like a .303" rifle bullet's cartridge, which caused a flash and that struck the bag of cordite and the explosive charge sent off the shell. The muzzle velocity depended on the amount of charge used. With that large gun, we used between one and five bags of cordite depending on the range at which the gun was to be fired.

The 7.2" howitzer was much simpler. It had a 200lb shell (about 90kg), which only needed two men to ram the shell home and then with the 155mm, my goodness, we had dropped. The shell weighed only 100lb (45kg), and one chap could ram it home into the barrel and that really would be a saving when we were in action.

There was one amusing incident at Hunstanton. The chaps were in billets, and at that time coal was rationed. The coal yard's store was behind a tall fence and just behind where our men were billeted. I jokingly said to some of them over a cup of tea: "If you blokes must go pinching coal, for god's sake don't get caught."

Of course one was caught. Was my face red. I had to appear in court as the 'soldier's friend' because he was charged with stealing. He said in his defence that he'd taken my joke seriously, and thought it was all right to go and pinch some coal provided he wasn't caught which, of course, he was. Anyway, the magistrates were pretty understanding. They let him off with a caution and then, with a twinkle in their eyes said to me: "We think you'd better be a bit more careful, Mainwaring, when you make these sorts of comments to your men." So that one was down to me.

While we were still at Hunstanton we had more mobile exercises. They were entirely on radio control and signal training, absolutely vital, and included a lot of moving the guns around. We'd hardly moved our 9.2" howitzers at all so we were a bit slow-minded at first.

We had to get used to getting these new 155mm guns into action quickly, camouflaging them and all that sort of thing. All quite new and interesting.

APRIL 1943 – SCRATCHING, SORE...HERTS

Around early April we pulled out of Hunstanton and moved to Hitchin in Hertfordshire before going up to Strensall near York in May for more exercises in the Yorkshire Dales, especially around Pickering.

All these moves were supposed to be secret. There was obviously some wit in the background who dreamed up the code name for Hitchin, Herts. It became 'Scratching, Sore'.

I was still battery captain in 25 Battery at Hitchin with Laurie Wass as battery commander. Hilary Bickford-Smith, who later became one of our first son's godparents, was the senior subaltern, and we had three other officers. Laurie Wass's wife was pregnant at the same time as Peggy, so when they met they had plenty to talk about.

We used to take our 155mm guns to the market square in Hitchin, just off the High Street, on non-market days and go through our gun drill in the square. A different place for gun drill was allocated to each of the four batteries of the regiment. My goodness, it was a noisy business.

Peggy and I managed to find somewhere to stay for a short time whilst we were at Hitchin. The lady of the house had a couple of Sealyham terriers. The poor things had some infection that made them frightfully smelly. I think they'd had it so long she no longer noticed. We certainly did.

In May we made the move to Strensall, near York.

JULY 1943 – BABY ARRIVED 6.10 p.m. BOY

While we were there, July came, and on the twenty-first a telegram arrived saying that our son Simon had been born. I still have the note in my writing case in the medieval chest at home where all those precious family documents live, just as I wrote it down: 'Baby arrived 6.10 pm. Boy. Both quite well. Weight 7lb 10 ozs.'

I got three days' leave when Peggy came out of Danbury Palace where Simon had been born, noting not everyone's born in a palace even if it was doubling as a maternity hospital.

Of course it was a most wonderful experience with the new baby, but it was made more difficult because Simon was what was known then as a 'colicky baby'. He cried a hell of a lot and didn't seem to be at all well. Peggy was getting pretty desperate. However, that was just one of the difficult things of life at the time that you just had to work your way through.

Initially Peggy had been working with the eccentric genius Stuart in North Fambridge who had invented this special system of threading very tough metal. After becoming pregnant, she moved to a job nearer to her family home at the Black Cottage in Langford. She worked at the Crittalls factory in Heybridge where she was trained in electric welding. As a qualified welder she made parts for anti-tank mines. She stayed there until the time came when she had to give up work.

A pretty tough job that electric welding was too. Dangerous on the eyes if you were careless, and you had to wear a mask. One of the things Peggy used to say was that the target of production set by the union, which was male-dominated, was exceeded by far by many of the women, including Peggy. Then when the bonuses were paid for extra work completed above the target, the highest percentage of the bonus by far, which was earned jointly by the men and the women, went to the men. It seemed to be grossly unfair that the women didn't get the real proportion that they had earned.

Sometimes today you hear about vast money being earned by munition workers during the war. Peggy was alternately doing a fortnight's night work and a fortnight's day work. It was a fifty-six-hour week, which sounds pretty grim now. But this was wartime. Her average wage was £2.12.6 for day and night work over the whole period she worked there. A pretty low figure and a long way from anyone's idea of vast money.

Thinking of Peggy and the lives of women in the war, and particularly the wives and girlfriends we loved, leads me to another parallel story.

One of my pre-war friends at Queens', Cambridge, R.B. Osborne, had been in the university air squadron and won the DSO during the war as the pilot of a Lysander. He flew secret agents over to France from RAF Stradishall, guided in at night by the torches of French Resistance fighters to land in small fields. RAF Stradishall is only 3 miles from our present home in Suffolk.

The agents were hidden away until the time came for them to be dropped into France in Batchelors Hall, which lies down a tiny lane within sight of RAF Stradishall, just outside the nearby village of Hundon. I believe it is more than likely that it was from Stradishall that Eliane Plewman and her brother were flown over to France to begin their activities as secret agents

STRENSALL

At Strensall we ran a series of mobile exercises, especially around the Pickering area, where I failed to be terribly sensible. One very wet day when we were on an exercise I'd got my OP team together. We travelled in a Bren gun carrier, which was a small low-profile tracked vehicle the OP parties used, and we were on our way back to base at the end of the exercise.

I rather fancied myself as a driver having been on a month's advanced M.T. course. One tends to be a bit too cocky when young. So I said to the proper driver: "I'll take over for a bit here."

I moved over into the driving seat. Fairly soon we went down a steep hill, the roads had cobbled surfaces, and came to a sharp left-hand bend.

The hill was steeper than I had realised. I was going far too fast and, as we went round the corner, the Bren carrier skidded to the right hard against the granite kerb and neatly took off the right-hand track. So there we were, with me the battery captain, stuck on a corner while the rest of the battery went past with plenty of pretty ribald comments.

Fortunately Tail-end Charlie, the recovery wagon, was the last vehicle in our column with our expert vehicle mechanic Bombardier Mountain aboard, who later deservedly became a sergeant. He stopped and successfully put the track back on the carrier.

"Very well done," I said. "I don't know how you managed it."

He looked at me with a twinkle in his eye and said: "Magic, Sir."

With the real driver back in his seat we headed back. That's how stupid you can be when showing off, because showing off invariably involves seriously over-estimating your competence.

Another mildly curious incident that sticks in the memory was when passing very close to York Minster at 3 a.m. in the cab of a Scammell tractor towing one of our huge guns back from a late night exercise. Heaven only knows how much vibration the convoy caused in the ancient minster. They were big hefty guns but we were going fairly slowly, so I hope it was all right. I don't suppose many people have driven past York Minster towing massive guns in the middle of the night.

But overall, by August 1943, ten months before the D-Day invasion, the tone of life was noticeably beginning to change and we knew before long we would seriously be going to war.

Our rather fierce brigadier, Archie Campbell, was a cracking chap, very keen on swift movement, quick reaction and proper control over your signalling equipment and wireless drill, all that sort of business. Very strict. He was due to come to do a big inspection of the regiment but before that, he sent us on a particular exercise and watched everything that we did. He came and inspected all of the guns and vehicles in our wagon lines.

Whilst the brigadier was going round on his inspection of the vehicles, my close friend Hilary Bickford-Smith wasn't going to have any nonsense standing around wasting time before the CAGRA (Commander Army Group, Royal Artillery) came along.

He thought he had time to do what's called a '406 inspection'. The number simply refers to the book in which details of each inspection is recorded. Every vehicle in the army has to have a full inspection once a month checking everything: brakes, engine points and all the rest of it.

When the brigadier got to one of the ammunition wagons, there was Hilary on his back, wearing a set of dirty old denims, inspecting all the necessary parts beneath the vehicle.

"What are you doing there?" Archie asked him.

Hilary was a pretty untidy chap at the best of times, a Wykehamist with a great sense of humour who'd read PPE (Politics, Philosophy & Economics) at New College, Oxford. He was a highly intellectual chap who never looked frightfully tidy. He came out from under the wagon, stood up straight, looked the CAGRA straight in the eye, and said: "Doing the necessary 406 on this vehicle, it's due today, sir."

In reply, the brigadier said: "Good for you, Bickford-Smith, I don't like to see people wasting their time. Far more sense doing that than standing around waiting for me. Good show," and off he went.

When we finally got to Normandy, Hilary was a man of great courage. He was awarded a Mention in Despatches for great bravery when trying to save his gunners' lives, and for seeing to their safety when his battery was badly shelled several times.

SUMMER 1943 – TIGHTENING AT THE TOP

A week after the CAGRA's inspection, of the four majors we had three were demoted, and three of the four captains demoted as well. The only two people who were not demoted were John Stone, who was commanding 8 Battery and, fortunately, me in 25 Battery, the only captain not demoted.

I don't know why they were demoted. I suppose for various reasons, perhaps they were thought not to be aggressive enough. I suppose the CAGRA needed to have commanding officers full of 'get up and go'. I expect he wanted a stiffening at the top, considering the only regular officer in the whole regiment was the commanding officer himself.

In the event, what the CAGRA did was to post in three regular army majors, all of whom had experience of war conditions in the Middle East and elsewhere. They were all jolly good officers. It was disappointing, of course, for those who had been demoted, but they'd all had a pretty quick promotions earlier.

Speaking for myself, it was probably a good job I hadn't been promoted to major earlier after all, in spite of my disappointment at the time. Laurie Wass, who'd replaced me as commanding officer of 25 Battery twenty-one days after I'd formed it in January of 1943, was also demoted.

John Stone remained as commanding officer of 8 Battery, but his battery captain was demoted and a new chap called Johnson was posted in from outside.

Turnbull, who had commanded 9 Battery, was demoted and posted away and was replaced by a very good regular officer, Hugh Sweetman. Jack Tremlett, battery captain of 9 Battery, was demoted and I was sidestepped and became battery captain with Hugh Sweetman. Hugh, coming in from outside, needed someone who knew the ropes in the regiment, and so from then on to the end of the European campaign I was battery captain of 9 Battery.

It was sad in a way to leave 25 Battery, but on the other hand 9 Battery was a top class battery and Hugh Sweetman was a good fellow, later on to be replaced by another regular officer, Peter Selfe, with whom I was still in touch in 2002.

For the time being, however, while we were there at Strensall, and later when we moved to Blyth in Nottinghamshire, Hugh and I were to get our batteries into shape.

In 24 Battery, Bernard Elkins was demoted, which was rather sad, although he remained as battery captain. Another regular major, James Brooksbank, came in as battery commander.

Laurie Wass remained in 25 Battery as battery captain, and Toby Welch was posted in as battery captain. So there were three new battery captains, all regulars: Hugh Sweetman in 9, James Brooksbank in 24, and Toby Welch in 25. John Stone remained as battery captain in 8, and I moved sideways into 9 Battery so that Laurie Wass could stay as battery captain of 25.

It all suggested a strong tightening at the top, putting in place the right people for a rigorous command structure capable of undertaking a massive co-ordinated operation of overwhelming force.

We knew what was coming.

Later on there was one odd coincidence but I can't imagine there was any significance in it beyond curiosity. During the

European campaign, the only two combatant officers in the regiment who hadn't been demoted and had been decorated were John and me.

He was the major not demoted and was later awarded the MC, and I was the captain not demoted, also later awarded the MC and twice Mentioned in Despatches. Hilary Bickford-Smith was also Mentioned in Despatches and he hadn't been demoted either. He wasn't a captain at the time but later became my battery captain when I was promoted to command 25 Battery after Toby Welch was posted to Burma.

Throughout the time at Strensall, camp life was taken up with mobile and other exercises. Radio exercises, camouflage, etc., all of which were absolutely essential.

Whilst I was at Strensall, I managed occasionally to get a forty-eight-hour leave, and came down to have a very brief stay with Peggy and the baby at the Black Cottage. I was able to take the train to Liverpool Street, and then up to Witham and Langford. Of course, wartime travel was very restricted and crowded.

OCTOBER 1943 – BLYTH

It must have been around the beginning of October 1943 when we moved south to Blyth in Nottinghamshire, just off the Great North Road, the A1. The battery's guns were in the grounds of Blyth Hall, a rather nice old Queen Anne house with lovely lawns and woods and with peacocks in the gardens. I was billeted in the rectory a few hundred yards from the hall.

All the talk then was of the second front. We knew that the invasion of Western Europe was going to come fairly soon, but of course we didn't know when. There was pressure from the Russians. Ever since the Dieppe raid in August 1942, they'd been pressing us, going on and on, saying the British were doing nothing. As far as we were concerned in England we were keyed up, but getting rather fed up because we were not seeing any action.

We knew it had to come sooner or later.

There had been Alamein in 1942 after the disasters in the Far East. I suppose we were feeling a bit guilty that we were still safe and sound in England. Nevertheless, we were preparing thoroughly for the invasion of Europe. As battery captain I was responsible for all the stores, replenishment of ammunition, etc., and seeing that all our stores for action, called 1098 stores, were fully supplied and checked. We practised packing and repacking everything into our battery transport. We had exercises getting the guns into action with all the stores packed in the best way for instant use. It was all very tedious really but it had to be repetitive so we could do it blindfold.

Everybody in the battery knew what his own particular job was, and how to do it to the best advantage. We knew it wasn't going to be easy, but we had to be ready to get on with it when things weren't so comfortable and you were being shelled or bombed. You had to be able to do things automatically.

AUTUMN 1943 – LIFE AND WAR STILL GO ON

Fortunately, and as always, family life carried on regardless of the demands of war, including the wedding of my cousin Joan, daughter of my Uncle Jacques who had been posted to RAF Wick in Coastal Command as adjutant with the RAF Volunteer Reserve, being ex-Royal Flying Corps.

Joan had joined the WAAF and was working on the plot table in Fighter Command during the Battle of Britain, logging enemy aircraft approaching. She was marrying my oldest friend, Foster

Robson, who I had known since we were 8 or 9. Robbie had won a MC as a glider pilot in the Sicily landings.

By a stroke of good fortune, when Joan and Robbie were about to get married I happened to go on a five-day gunnery equipment course at Hanley, in the Potteries. When the course ended I was able to go to their wedding at my pre-war home church, St Margaret's, Dunham Massey near Altrincham, before I went back to the battery.

Robbie had managed to get special leave. His best man was another very old friend of us both, Flight Lieutenant Alan Crabtree. Sadly, Alan was lost in a Hudson over the Atlantic in Coastal Command. No one ever knew what happened to the plane. Many years later, after Peggy had begun her magnificent collection of twelfth scale dolls' houses, she bought a dolls' house shop to add to it as it had the name Crabtree on the shopfront. We fitted it out completely to commemorate Alan.

Robbie was in the Arnhem landings. During the battle his leg was broken and he was taken prisoner. It was pretty rough. Joan knew where he was as a prisoner-of-war, at Kassel. She tried to tell me where he was in some sort of code, which I was never able to decipher. I never knew where he was until I saw him when he had been released after the war.

Uncle Jacques was by then a squadron leader and when I was chatting to him at the wedding he told me that he had moved to HQ, No.1 Bomber Group at Bawtry, which was only 4 miles from my battery at Blyth. So, when we had both returned to our units after the wedding, he asked me over for dinner at the RAF mess at Bawtry. After dinner he showed me some of their extraordinary 3D photos. I'd never seen that type of photo before, taken by RAF recce planes after bombing raids. It was a real eye-opener. They showed the incredible destruction and bomb damage over in Germany. The WAAF officers were very expert in interpreting these photographs, and you could really see with their magnifying instruments just exactly what had happened.

Peggy:
One time I was stuck in London. I couldn't get out because of an air-raid. I was ushered into a sub-basement in Wardour Street, it was a basement below a basement. I felt far more unsafe, all these great pipes and things, and it was full, you know what Soho's like: full of all the nations of the world. And they were all still going down into this already full sub-basement. I'd much rather have risked the bombs out in the open air.

...THE DOGS... 4

SPRING 1944 – TRAINING AND LIFE INTENSIFY

As time went by in the autumn of 1943 and over Christmas and spring 1944, we had more and more training as an AGRA. We had a lot of exercises together with the other regiments of the AGRA. Sometimes these were just signals exercises with the officers controlling the fire in practice shoots over their radios. We had to get the radio drills right.

There were also exercises with all the vehicles out, and with our fellow regiments: 25 Field; 61st, 63rd, & 77th (Duke of Lancaster's Own Yeomanry) Medium regiments. It was not only essential experience, we also got to know the other chaps with their strengths and weaknesses, special abilities, and so on.

I managed to get one interesting break with a couple of days off duty. One of my friends in one of the other regiments was going down to some course in London by road in a Dodge wagon, an American vehicle of a type we used to call a 'Gin Palace', a tall slim vehicle with left-hand drive. He offered to drop me off at the Black Cottage at Langford on his way down, and to pick me up on his way back. All the signposts had been removed in 1940 during the invasion scares, so we headed off through the snow having to find our route by map-reading all the way down. It was quite fun really, not to mention even more map-reading practice.

I had a very happy and unexpected break for forty-eight hours with Peggy and little Simon at the Black Cottage. My pal picked me up again on the way back from his course and dropped me off at Blyth on his way up north.

During the Spring of 1944, Peggy managed to come up to the Old Bell Hotel at Barnby Moor on the old A1, only a few miles away from Blyth. She brought Simon with her, a tricky journey by train in those days. I remember my batman Jock Flynn took a real shine to Simon, and Simon took a shine to him too. He was by then able to have hot milk to drink, and Peggy had to try to heat the milk over an old oil stove in their bedroom. Very difficult it was too. How on earth Peggy managed to get up there complete with pram, cot and bedding I have no idea, but it was wonderful that she actually managed it.

As winter moved into spring, it was clear the invasion of France was getting closer. We had a very big exercise put on by Monty (General Bernard Montgomery), *Exercise Eagle*, all over the Yorkshire Moors and into Lancashire. On this exercise we were attached to the 8th (British) Corps. That was the corps with which we would work once the landings had taken place. The whole of 8 AGRA, of which we were a part, would provide extra gunner support wherever needed. We were army troops and could be sent anywhere within the area of the Second Army when the commanding generals needed a special concentration of artillery fire.

All our training in the months before D-Day was done with the 8th Corps. Before going to Normandy, our time was spent on various exercises at battery regiment or AGRA level. They were all very useful because you constantly learned more and more about everybody's strengths, weaknesses and qualities. You were able to choose the best drivers, signallers and OP Acks. It would be so important when we went into action in France that we should have ready the best chaps, for example, in the Bren carriers in which we went up on OP duty. You really had to have good imperturbable men when you went to the OP.

Sven Berlin was my favourite OP Ack. He was steady as a rock and a well-known artist. He could draw superb panoramas of the enemy areas seen from an OP.

Of the battery's six officers, four were normally at the gun position. Jack Tremlett was the GPO with the three subalterns, whilst the battery captain and commanding officer shared the duties as OP officer.

Whilst we had been at Blyth, the commanding officer had been Hugh Sweetman, but later on, in the spring of 1944, as previously mentioned, Hugh was replaced by Peter Selfe, a regular major. Hugh was a very decent fellow who I liked very much, but personally I felt he was not really dynamic enough for a battery commander in the field. He was sent off to another regiment as a battery captain.

Now we had a substantive major in command. An excellent chap. We hit it off straight away and got on very well together, and we stayed together right through the campaign in north-west Europe. Altogether, we had a pretty good team, ready for anything.

I did most of my OP duties later on when we got into Normandy with Sven Berlin as my OP Ack, and Blanchard and Tonks. They were both drivers and signallers and between them they could do all the driving and signalling we would ever need. Terrific fellows.

When I wasn't at the OP but doing my duties as battery captain, I had a very good Scottish chap named Paterson, excellent in every way and a first class driver for my K truck. This was the vehicle for the second-in-command of a battery. My batman, who saw to my gear and so on, had been the jovial Jock Flynn since Blyth, so we got to know each other very well.

MAY 1944 – D-DAY: THE BUILD-UP GROWS

Exercise Eagle was the last big exercise we had before D-Day, and the months before that were used for more and more training. Then, during May, the invasion forces were gradually assembled in the south of England, and we went from Blyth down to Aldershot. We were distributed within a large area of barracks called Buller Barracks.

All through May, Monty was speaking in theatres and cinemas, first of all to the officers of what was then called the 'British Liberation Army', then later he went round into open fields where complete units were got together in semi-circular formation. He'd drive up in his Jeep and get up onto the bonnet and say, "Gather round, chaps," and everyone would do exactly that.

It was all quite exciting because as officers we had heard Monty twice. On the first occasion we heard him, all our regiment officers and officers from the rest of our AGRA of five Royal Artillery regiments went to a cinema somewhere in Aldershot. There, Monty unfolded the whole plan of the invasion using a huge map at the back of the stage. Of course, after we'd been told all these plans, there was no more getting away from our concentration areas because there might have been leaks. Careless talk, for example, in a pub, that sort of thing. I remember those famous cartoons by Fougasse with pictures of Hitler with a huge ear, listening in.

Just before we went to hear Monty, I was able to go up to Waterloo for one or two evenings in the first couple of weeks at Aldershot, and Peggy came up from Langford. We met at a restaurant in Oxford Street while Peggy's mum looked after Simon, and we had a couple of precious hours together in the early evening before she went back to the Black Cottage and I went back to Aldershot.

Monty's explanation of the whole plan with this huge map at the back of the stage was quite masterful. He showed us that a firm base ashore would be rapidly established. The Master Plan was that the British and Canadians would draw the German Army towards Caen. This would give the US troops to the west on our right the opportunity to break out from the Cotentin Peninsula once they'd taken Cherbourg.

The idea was that they'd first go south through the German crust, as it were, and then they'd turn east and sweep past the south of us whilst we carried on keeping the German armour fully engaged. The marvellous thing was that it all worked to the time schedule that Monty gave us. Of course, the newspapers kept grumbling that we were held up at Caen, saying we were too slow, why didn't we break out, and so on, but that was the whole idea.

Naturally, that couldn't be revealed openly anyway because it would let the Germans in on what was happening. Looking back, now that we know more about other aspects of the plan, Monty didn't speak about the deception, which of course we weren't told about either. There were full signal communications in Kent and East Anglia as if the whole of the invasion was going to take place in the Pas de Calais. So we knew where we were going. But we weren't told about the idea that the Germans were really going to be kept round the Pas de Calais area because of this other terrific plan, where radio communications were going on between fictitious units that were supposedly going to land there. It was a brilliant effort.

Needless to say, we didn't know anything about ULTRA (cryptographic intelligence), which was revealed in 1987/8. We had broken the codes of the Germans and Japanese, and we knew a lot of what they were planning. What was difficult was that we had to make our plans for our activities in such a way that we didn't reveal to the enemy that we knew what they were about.

Meanwhile, we carried on with our preparations for the invasion, as D-Day was getting nearer. We didn't know exactly when it would be, but we knew it had to be dependent on the weather. We got on with the waterproofing of our vehicles. That was a hell of a task. There were also several jobs that had to be done at the last minute. Collecting petrol, that sort of thing.

The main thing was that all our vehicles had to be waterproofed in such a way that they could go off the ramps from the barges or landing ships or whatever it was that we should eventually put aboard into up to 4 foot 6 inches or 5 feet of water (up to 1.5m). Amongst other things, that meant extending the exhaust pipe, protecting all the electrical components, etc. All a very tricky business and a filthy job. Quite apart from all these extensions, and so on, we had to use this sticky black mastic everywhere. You couldn't run the engines for very long with all the waterproofing in place without them becoming overheated. The plan was that once we were ashore we would go to an assembly area fairly near the beach, and there we would de-waterproof. When the time came that is exactly what happened.

We were in our area in Buller Barracks in Aldershot when we heard the news that D-Day had finally come, and we were all very excited about that. We knew we were going into Normandy fairly late-ish because VIII Corps, to which we were attached for gun support, was going to go in as the next major reinforcement once the beaches had been cleared and the bridgehead had been established. We moved south to our concentration area, which was in woods near a place called Buckler's Hard, which I think is well known to yachtsmen but I'd never heard of it before. It was somewhere, I think, a couple of miles south of Beaulieu Abbey and the west bank of the Beaulieu River, facing across the Solent towards Cowes on the north-west coast of the Isle of Wight.

Actually, it all became rather claustrophobic because we were confined to our battery area in these woods. No phone calls were allowed out and we, the officers, had to start censoring the mail. My

OP Ack, Sven Berlin, was a St Ives group sculptor and artist who later became well-known along with Ben Nicholson and Barbara Hepworth. He was a poet too and a remarkable man in every way. He always brought his letters to me to censor. He was a deep and thoughtful type, and wrote long philosophical letters to his wife. All through the fighting period I felt quite honoured that he came and asked me to read through and clear his very personal letters.

This reminded me of the never-ending bond that exists between comrades-in-arms who have faced the worst together. After an article of mine in *Gunner Magazine* in November 1994, fifty years after D-Day, I was contacted by several members of my old battery. Through them I was able to contact Sven, as well as my old CO of 9 Battery, Peter Selfe. Sven sadly died aged 89 in 1999. I am still in touch with Peter Selfe who, at the time of writing, is now aged 89, whilst I am now still a young man at 82.

5 ...OF WAR

6 JUNE 1944 – D-DAY: THE NORMANDY LANDINGS

Then the time came.

The waiting had seemed endless. It was not until 21 June that word came that we were to go. It was D+15 by then and we seemed to have waited for ever. They hadn't got inland from their beaches as quickly as they'd hoped and it had proved much more difficult than expected. Of course, Monty knew it wouldn't be easy, but the press were all saying: "They should have got further by now." But it wasn't as simple as it sounded.

There had to be room for VIII Corps to deploy, and to deploy a huge body of troops of all sorts, engineers, gunners and everything else. You really need plenty of space. By then all our vehicles had been waterproofed and all the stores were loaded. Even the order of loading aboard our landing craft had to be very carefully worked out so that if we needed to go into action quickly, the important things that would get the guns into action would be off-loaded in the right order.

Our stores had been checked and double-checked. Eventually we were taken onboard a landing ship tank (LST). It was one of those big landing craft, not quite a tanker, more of a cargo ship made by, ironically, Kaisers of America, who had a big rolling programme of ship-building.

Of course, many ships had been lost to U-Boat action in the Atlantic. To get these ships ready to embark all these troops for what was, after all, the biggest invasion in history, was a terrific enterprise. We were given our seasick pills and we sailed at dusk. It was quite a funny feeling looking at the shores of England as they faded in the distance, wondering if we'd be alive to get back again afterwards. I was one of the lucky ones.

Early next morning, we queued up to land with scores of RAF planes flying ahead with white recognition stripes painted under their wings.

As we were approaching close to the Normandy beaches, it was quieter than we expected. We didn't know as yet how far inland our chaps had got, though once we'd made it ashore we found out soon enough.

We had our maps issued, down went the ramps and, funnily enough, we landed virtually dry. In the event, all our waterproofing had not been necessary. Darned nuisance having to get rid of it all after we'd landed. The Beach Masters, Royal Navy fellows, got us cleared off the beaches as quickly as possible.

22 JUNE 1944 – JUNO BEACH

We landed on Juno Beach.

It was 22 June, near the once-peaceful seaside village of Courseulles-sur-Mer.

We were guided through white tape the sappers had laid to show that the tracks were cleared of mines. There was a terrible stink of dust all the time, which was constantly with us in this part of Normandy near the beaches.

Eventually we got to our first assembly area for de-waterproofing, predictably a very filthy job. We got the foul sticky muck off our vehicles and then we were all set to go. From there we were given our orders to go to our first gun position.

This was when a potentially disastrous oversight in our training hit us for the first time. All our exercises in England had been done with the good old 1 inch to the mile Ordnance Survey (OS) maps we were all used to. These were to a smaller scale than 1/50,000 scale of the French maps, which we had never used during our training. When you're reading a map you get used to the distances on the ground relating to the space on the map. With 1/50,000 maps being a bigger scale, quite a number of people initially got themselves in a mess because they had not gone as far as they thought due to the scale difference.

Also, all the roads in France were marked on the maps in a slightly different way from the way we were used to. To my mind, looking back, this was predictable and avoidable. I think an awful lot of people went astray, getting lost, missing rendezvous, etc., all because of this difference in the maps. Why the devil couldn't we have had the 1" OS maps translated to a 1/50,000 scale for our exercises in the UK, with the same markings as we would have when we got into France? Then we would have become used to it, and it would have been far less confusing, and far safer.

That really is one of my serious criticisms of the planning, but one that, in our case, fortunately didn't end badly.

I was battery captain, second-in-command of the battery, and was given the area of the gun position. My job was to get the battery over to that position.

Peter Selfe, our battery commander, had gone off to recce an OP because we were then, of course, doing our best to move south. Accordingly, we went from this area near Courseulles to our first gun position at a tiny village called St Croix Grande Tonne. From here we began firing our guns in earnest at the opening of the Battle of the Odon. (image 12)

The Battle of the Odon was part of an operation I have since learned was Operation *Epsom*, but we didn't know that at the time. We knew what our job was with the guns.

I certainly remember the first night there. I slept in a ditch. At that point we hadn't had much time for digging slit trenches and there weren't very many dug. Luckily, we were not shelled in that position, so we got away with it.

24 JUNE 1944 – THE BATTLE OF THE ODON

Very shortly after we got to the gun position, on the evening of 24 June, the battle began with the aim of crossing the River Odon. Three divisions were involved. There was the 15th (Scottish) Division we'd trained quite a lot with, the 43rd (Wessex) Division, and also the 11th Armoured Division. They were all highly trained and determined divisions.

In this battle for the Odon, one or two things were done for which we had not trained that maybe we should have thought of, similar to the situation with the maps. Typically, with our move to the first gun position at St Croix Grande Tonne, it was more by luck than judgement that I got us there. I was as unaccustomed to the 1/50,000 map as anyone else, but fortunately we made it. It was just darned lucky really.

Early in the Battle of the Odon, there was one major from each of the AGRA regiments who went up to find themselves OP positions. It was a disastrous experiment. They were each given a Sherman tank to go forward with the attacking 11th Armoured Division tanks. What was so stupid was that the OP tanks went with their lids up when the attacking tanks did not, so the Germans knew they were obviously OPs. Instead of going in our little Bren gun carriers, which look like any other Bren carrier and are not obviously a gunner OP, there they were. Tanks with their lids up with the officers' heads clearly visible, searching for targets with their binoculars.

Out of the five majors who went on this disastrous attack three were killed by snipers. They were the targets. We hadn't practised this anywhere. Luckily for us John Stone, who I mentioned earlier, one of my great buddies who by then was commanding officer of 8 Battery, was untouched and jolly glad to get back too, I can tell you. We didn't do any of that again.

So that was a lesson sadly, disastrously and stupidly learned, I think. I don't know why the devil it was done, but sometimes these things happen. Someone has a bright idea they didn't think through, some high-ranking officer somewhere who should have been, and maybe was, rightly carpeted. It was idiotic, not least because there had to be changes in those batteries whose commanders were killed. You should be able to deal with situations after casualties I know, but it did mean changes that should not have been necessary.

In future, when we went up on OP duty, we went in our little Bren gun carriers. You couldn't take your Bren gun carrier onto the skyline, you had to leave it somewhere out of sight. We had a remote-control device with half-a-mile of cable you just reeled out behind you, well-oiled, of course, so it didn't squeak or make any noise. You crawled out and made your way to the best position you could find for your OP within half-a-mile of the Bren carrier, and then you were relatively safe from snipers. If you'd got any sense or at least the will to live, you kept your head low and didn't stick it up in full view of the enemy.

JULY 1944 – TIGERS AT CARPIQUET

Having got over this last disaster, we were back to our Bren gun carriers. I then, of course, had to take my turn at OP duty alternating with Peter Selfe. Thank god I didn't have to go up in a Sherman tank. I kept to my little old Bren carrier. One of the tricky jobs we had to do around then was in the area of Carpiquet aerodrome, near Caen.

I haven't got any of my maps from those days, so I can't really check where everything was, but Carpiquet aerodrome was an absolute menace to us. It was still in the hands of the Luftwaffe, and it was defensively surrounded by German Tiger tanks dug in, hull down and, of course, they were pretty dangerous things. They were difficult to get at, and difficult to take out, so it was decided that the best thing to do was to try to pick them off with our heavy guns.

The job fell to me as one of my first jobs when my turn came for OP duty. I needed to find somewhere in the Carpiquet area, which was all fairly flat, from which I could get a view of these Tiger tanks, dug in. All you could see was their turrets.

I had to find a suitable place and take the remote control out of the carrier, in fact almost to the very end of the cable, half-a-mile nearly. We then had Sven and myself at the actual OP hoping they didn't spot us, with the other two, Blanchard and Tonks, back in the carrier working the switches on the remote control while we were controlling the fire. Actually, it was rather like a training exercise but with a substantially more dangerous target. I had to try to pick them off one by one. And we did it. But it was a very tricky business.

My OP Ack Sven Berlin had the job at the OP to draw a panorama of what we could see from the position. On the panorama would be marked all the salient features, and we would also enter the estimate from our map-reading of the bearing and distance from the guns to these features. With that as a guide, we then 'ranged' on to our chosen target.

You have to imagine the line of fire from the guns to the target, i.e. exactly where the shell will travel. Also, you must take into account what is called the 'hundred per cent zone', which is a cigar-shaped area probably 150 yards long by 15 yards wide into which the shells will fall. Out of every 100 shells at a set range, half will fall within 20 yards plus or minus, and 5 yards right or left of the target. Having 'bracketed' the target with a shell, then making adjustments for plus and minus relative to the ranging shell, on the correct line, you then go to 'fire for effect' and hope to hit it.

I think we were jolly lucky in picking off these tanks one by one, and eventually we had an almost incredible bag when we managed to get nine of them. It was all a pretty exciting thing really, seeing the shells coming down near and then right on top of a very valuable enemy target, one after another. Fortune was certainly smiling on us that day because, somehow, they didn't spot us, and we managed to get up there for the OP and back in one piece. We could certainly claim a few more than one-up to us on that occasion. We found out later that the aerodrome was in the hands of the RAF not long after, so that was a handy little job.

MOVING SOUTH

By this time Monty had drawn the bulk of the German armour against us. In terms of numbers, if I remember rightly, there were something like 700 German tanks against us to the east of Caen and that only left them with about 200 against the Americans in the Cotentin peninsula. In theory, at least the Americans should have had an easier job in breaking out.

Having knocked out Carpiquet aerodrome we then tried to press further south. I remember several OP jobs I had. We seemed to be constantly passing over the road from Bayeux to Caen at one little village called Bretteville I'Orgueilleuse and another called St Leger. I think it was Bretteville I'Orgueilleuse where we crossed more often, going south through a village called Cheux.

There was a very sad sight in Cheux. The road went within a few yards of an old French farmhouse and, hanging out of an upstairs window with his stomach torn to bits was the body of a kilted Scottish soldier. Of course, nobody had been able to get in to retrieve the body as the house was mined and booby-trapped. His poor broken body was still there each time as we went by, three or four times, on our way to an OP. When I revisited Normandy in 1994, fifty years later, I laid a Royal British Legion poppy at the gate of the farmhouse in his memory.

All the time there was the dust. Another smell I always had in my mind throughout Normandy was of burning houses and the smell of scorched timbers. Then too there were dead animals around, cattle that had not been milked, and horses that had been killed by shellfire. Their poor bodies had become full of gases, a most unpleasant and sad business.

Again, I can't remember all the details of the area but Hill 112 was one of those spots the Germans held and we had to get them off it, so we were involved in that battle too. In the end we succeeded in disposing of them. In his letter of 1994 Sven says of Hill 112: 'I remember that expedition as one of the toughest' (see appendix).

By now we had been ashore for about a fortnight and we were still up around Caen. From our gun position we were able to watch the Lancasters and Halifaxes coming over and bombing Caen. We could actually see the bombs leaving the planes and great clouds of dust coming up along the horizon. Caen itself was smashed to bits, except for the cathedral, which somehow miraculously escaped with hundreds of people sheltering there. Shades of St Paul's surviving the bombing of London in the Blitz.

By then we'd pinpointed a lot of enemy tanks in other places. One of our jobs was to locate targets even if we didn't actually take them on at the time. Once the bombing of Caen was over, around 7 July, we laid on an all-night barrage by all the guns of the AGRA. This was a continuous shoot against all the pinpointed tanks we'd spotted. In the end, with our massed gunfire, we destroyed something like sixty-five out of 150 tanks the Germans had there. That was another one-up to the gunners.

A couple of days later, by 9 July, Carpiquet aerodrome itself was fully in our hands. Of course, the RAF could then commandeer it as their forward aerodrome and use their rocket-firing Typhoons for sorties, giving close ground attack support to advancing troops.

Following that, we were moved round to the east of Caen with the Canadians. Our AGRA went into the Canadian area to break up the big concentrations of German tanks. We had another all-guns shoot, and knocked out more tanks. This was quite rewarding and we felt we'd achieved something.

One unfortunate incident involved the continual bombing that was going on. The Canadians had borrowed some American Mitchell bombers. Sadly, as they came over, they bombed our battery and several others nearby by mistake thinking we were Germans. They'd obviously got their map-reading badly wrong and so we took some unnecessary casualties there. Awful when you think of it, but I suppose 'friendly fire' is one more of the tragic things that happens in war.

Once we'd got to Caen we moved back, away from the Canadians. Odd names come to mind now. Caumont and Villers Bocage especially, they were very rough places. There was an awful corner, where we turned off left to go to the OP, called Sept Vents, or Seven Winds. There was an awful stench on that corner of dead animals, cattle and horses. It haunts me to this day, the poor things lying there greatly inflated and, for some, their bodies had collapsed, the gases having escaped. You were prepared to kill the enemy, but to see these poor animals all dead around the fields was terrible.

There really was no abating. We were twenty-four hours in an area and then we would move on a bit. We were continually pressing on wherever we were required.

Around this time, 21 July was getting closer, Simon's first birthday. So, not knowing how long the mail would take to get home, I drew a little birthday card for him and got all the chaps in my K truck to sign it, and I sent it off to Peggy at the Black Cottage, hoping it would get there in time for his first birthday, little feller.

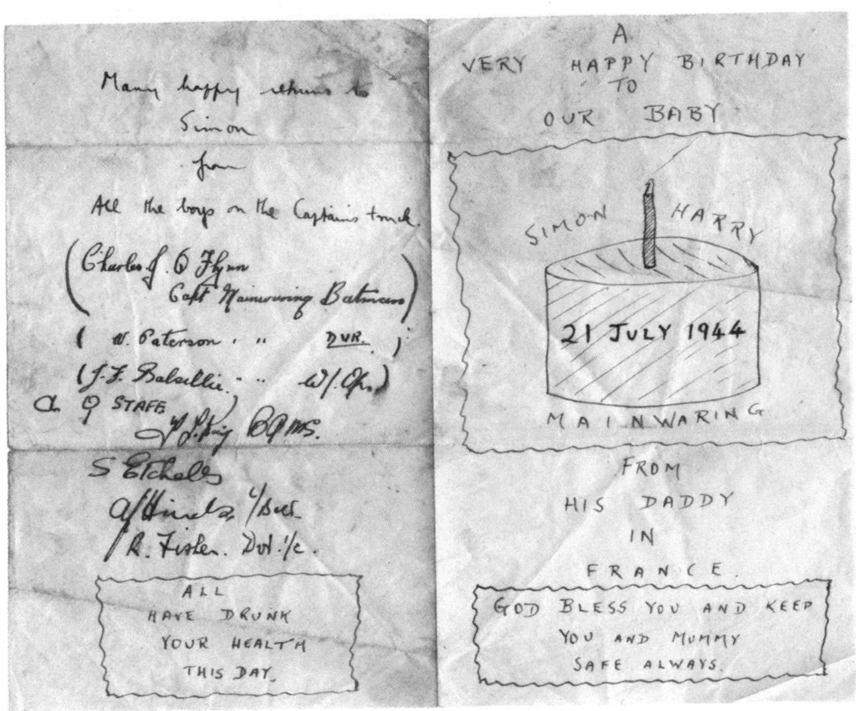

It says a lot for the army's preparedness and organisation, because it did actually arrive in good time, even in these fast-moving front line circumstances.

SEEING PHANTOMS

I had various jobs in the Normandy campaign. I was not only doing duties as battery captain and alternating with Peter Selfe at the OP, but from time to time I also had quite a number of jobs to do as a liaison officer. That was perhaps because I was in a rather unique position in the regiment because I had been adjutant. Also, John Stone, who had preceded me as adjutant, was now a battery commander and couldn't be spared. I was a battery captain and, as such, it was 'fair-do's' to take me away from battery duty when necessary and use me as a regimental liaison officer.

It was an extraordinarily interesting job and right on the pulse of the action. Whilst acting as a liaison officer, I frequently had to visit the 'Phantom' tents. To explain the Phantom, the members of this group wore on their arm a black shield emblazoned with a white letter 'P', and they were in fact the Northamptonshire Yeomanry. In Normandy, they were Monty's eyes and ears.

Montgomery believed in getting absolutely up-to-the-minute accurate information as well as what he received over the radio. These young Phantom officers dashed about to see with their own eyes what was really happening on the ground and reported back direct to him. They were all very brave and experienced officers and in their caravans or, more frequently, in large tents or marquees they had large-scale maps showing the whole of the front, all marked up with the actual positions of our own troops and those of the enemy.

As the battle unfolded you could see where all the concentrations were coming from and how Monty's master plan was coming into fruition. It really was quite clear that once the Americans started their dash down the Cotentin Peninsula they were in for a good run when they turned to the east.

It was exciting and fascinating. During our earlier exercises from Blyth, I had been called in from the battery to help out in RHQ, and I'd gone out then on exercises as a liaison officer. I'd seen a lot of the chaps I met later in Normandy in the 6th Guards Tank Brigade when they had been based at Welbeck Abbey. The old house there now is where young officer cadets are trained for entry to the specialist corps, such as the REME (Royal Electrical and Mechanical Engineers), RAOC, etc. I met people there who later became quite well-known, such as politician Willie Whitelaw, and Bob Runcie, who became Archbishop of Canterbury in 1980, and who got a very well-deserved MC in the north-west Europe campaign. I also met a number of people who I got to know quite well when later, in 1955/7 as a post-war regular officer, I was on the staff of the HQ of the Household Brigade at London District.

Whilst carrying out my duties as a liaison officer, I had my first experience of being shelled by those very nasty Nebelwerfers. They had a six-chambered revolving barrel that fired quite heavy mortar shells. I'd gone on a job liaising with HQ 129 Brigade, one of the 15 (Scottish) Division's brigades. No sooner had I arrived there than I had to dive into a slit trench very quickly, because these Nebelwerfers opened up, shelling all around the area of the brigade HQ. That showed without any doubt that getting into a slit trench as quickly as possible was a very good idea and pretty safe, except from a direct hit.

TANK TRAP

Near the beaches, and certainly as far as we'd got at this point, there was a lot of apple orchard country, interspersed with the odd field of corn. On one occasion I'd had to go to some OP earlier on, which was pretty hairy because the only way I could get through to it was across a cornfield that had been mined. Rather foolhardily, I suppose, we went across it, Harry Tonks driving the Bren carrier and me walking in front of it, looking as closely as I could at the roots of the corn. It wasn't very high, not yet a good crop, and I felt we'd see any disturbances where mines had been planted. Perhaps that was a bit risky in retrospect. However, we managed to get across safely. Sometimes you just had to do these things if you were to get the job done.

I had an OP on little Simon's first birthday, 21 July, near a village called Le Mesnil-Patry. It was a miserable day, the wet making every track muddy and slithery. The Bren carrier didn't like the mud all that much, which was unfortunate because you were very often not on roads but going across or around fields. It was a filthy day, and I felt rotten. We brewed up some sort of quick lunch at midday. We'd got one of those army tins of pork and something frightfully fatty. I don't think I've ever been so sick. It was absolutely appalling, I didn't feel at all well.

Not feeling well wasn't really much help, because just then we were in the middle of an operation called, I think, 'Goodwood'. We'd just had a pretty rough time. I think about 100 of our tanks had been destroyed by the Germans. Their Tiger tanks were more than a match for anything we'd got. I can't quite recall where we were attacking at the time, but we knew there was a concentration of German tanks somewhere.

However, once beyond Le Mesnil-Patry, we were cautiously moving forward in the Bren carrier along one of those deep country roads you have in the Bocage countryside of Normandy, hedges on the embankments on both sides of what was not much more than a cart track, looking for enemy targets to shoot up.

Very luckily, I managed to catch sight of about sixty German tanks that were 'laagering', partly concealed in a fold in the land. The position was hidden on higher ground not too far away from the main road between Bayeux and Caen, where our troops were having problems with a great deal of resistance when advancing towards Caen. It was getting late in the day by then, but they'd gone to laager for the night pretty early. I suppose it was about 7 p.m. by then. (image 17)

It was an ideal spot we'd got into. I had the remote control out, Sven was with me, and we had a lovely view of these tanks.

So I called for an AGRA shoot. That was for over 100 guns, all concentrating their fire on this close area. And, wet or not, feeling lousy or not, the shoot went very well. Actually, it was rather like an exercise. Everything couldn't have worked better. There was this gathering, I think I counted sixty-one or sixty-two tanks, and we made a real mess of that concentration.

I don't know quite how many we destroyed or damaged, but they were only 300 or 400 yards away from us and our shells were coming in from all over the place, and getting uncomfortably close to us as well. We felt we'd done our bit so perhaps we didn't really stay as long as we might have done, but we certainly did massive damage to that lot. They started moving away but we'd definitely had something of a proper impact.

MOVING ON

From this point, until we were taken out of action some time after we'd captured Flers on 16 August, things began to move rather slowly at first and then slightly more quickly as the Battle of the Falaise Gap began to take place, and the Germans were trapped.

Beyond the world of our activities the war was progressing across a wide front. Fairly soon after our tank-busting OP on Simon's birthday the Americans broke out through St Lo and the Cotentin peninsula, and they were able to pass through Avranches.

To try to stop them, the Germans attacked westwards towards Mortain with about 250 tanks, a pretty big effort. That was all the tanks they'd managed to gather together coming up from the south-east. It was a failure.

We could now begin to feel that success was coming. Knowing what Monty's plan had been, we were looking forward to really beginning to move. At this point we had no idea what a great success this was all going to lead to in the end.

In the middle of August, once the Americans had got down to Avranches, they could move slightly more south-east and then east. The Canadians were still east of Caen, to the east of us. Both they and us could therefore now move southwards. In the end, that would be the pincer movement that would trap the Germans in the middle, between Falaise in the north and Argentan in the south. That was where the trap was going to come.

In our own bigger picture, we moved forward through a place called St Martin des Besaces, where I had a rather disastrous OP action, and then we advanced on to Vire, and then eventually further on to Tinchebray and Flers, where we were taken out of the line for a bit of relaxation. By then it was the middle of August and we'd been in the thick of the action continually from 22 June when we landed right up to 16 August. That was quite a long haul.

Peggy:

I was going home to Essex by train from London one night. I was holding the baby as we rattled slowly along with all these railway lines side by side around us. Suddenly the air-raid sirens wailed and the train came to a stop, I suppose because the sparks from the engine could be seen from the air. So there we were, stuck in the middle of the East End and all of a sudden this shower of flares, incendiary bombs, were falling all round us.

There were rows of old houses, they were real slums in those days. They had some sort of lamp bracket or street lamps outside, and these incendiaries used to hang on those and catch on everything, lighting up the place and setting fire to anything that would burn, buildings, anything.

There we were, sat in the middle of the railway line in a train, stopped, in an air-raid, with incendiary bombs flaring away all around us. If you could get out and run you'd probably be better off. I was sitting there in the frightened hush of the railway carriage, everybody holding their breath, with little Simon in my arms. He was now beginning to use a few words and his little voice broke the silence: "Oh buggers." The tension seemed to break and people couldn't help but laugh. Talk about Blitz spirit. It was a huge relief when the train started again.

There was one man in the East End, he was in bed and a bomb hit somewhere close by. The blast wrapped his mattress around him and chucked him out the window. He was all right though.

A CLOSE RUN THING

Naturally enough, throughout that period it is the details that paint the personal pictures you hold in your memory, always the details. Our OP at St Martin des Besaces, mentioned earlier, was definitely one of these.

Our particular part of the front line was to the north-west of St Martin des Besaces when I had to go ahead to do an OP. Our route was along a road with a railway line running parallel to it just to the north. We had got about 3 or 4 miles to the west of St Martin des Besaces, and our front line hadn't yet reached this far. Infuriatingly, at this point our radio set in the Bren carrier went 'off net', leaving us in bandit country without communications.

So we stopped. Neither Tonks nor Blanchard seemed able to get the set back onto the net so I said: "I'll have a go," and got into the back of the carrier to try to retune the radio.

Meanwhile, I said to Sven Berlin: "You take us on for a while, you know where we're going."

After some time I was lucky enough to get the radio back, and we were in contact with the battery again, as we ought to be. When we returned to our normal places in the carrier, I asked Sven to point out to me where we were on the map. This he did, but unfortunately he didn't get our location quite right.

This goes back to something I mentioned earlier about the ghastly mistakes that could happen when we were using these 1/50,000 maps as opposed to the good old 1 inch to the mile scale we'd trained on in England. And Sven, for all his extraordinary talents as an OP Ack, drawing panoramas and so on, possibly wasn't the world's best map-reader.

At this point he told me we were at point X, as it were, with the railway running parallel with us, which it was, but he must have missed noticing a track or back road going off the road we were rolling along. The truth was we'd gone far further than we thought so I was looking for various things to appear, as you do when you're looking ahead on the map. And then, virtually before we could gather our wits we were at the crossroads in the middle of St Martin des Besaces. (images 19 and 20)

We had just rounded a short but sharp left hand bend when we burst onto this crossroads, and it suddenly dawned on me.

"My god – we shouldn't be here."

There had been no sign of life earlier but as we got to the crossroads, there over to the right was a whole bloody great convoy of Germans brewing up their lunch. I shouted to Harry Tonks: "Left here. LEFT – QUICK!"

That should have taken us right back to our own lines, but god knows where it was really heading, possibly on to more ravenous Germans.

We couldn't turn round and go back, and straight ahead over the crossroads as we got there were loads more German vehicles that had just come into view as well.

So with as much haste as we could muster, and Tonks' foot hard down on the floor, we swung round to the left. Luckily, before too far, the road weaved a bit further left and later curved slightly to the right, so we were more or less out of sight of the crossroads. A few shots chased us, but it doesn't say much for the alertness of the Germans' pickets.

As if this shave wasn't close enough, the next problem was rapidly approaching because, of course, somehow we had to get back to our own lines. So we turned the Bren carrier left-handed off the road and on to open country. We were going fairly well uphill and hopefully heading for home.

As we were going back up towards our own lines, naturally enough we were spotted by our own people. Since we were approaching from the wrong direction, they must have thought the Germans were suddenly putting on a surprise attack using a captured British Bren carrier in the van. So they began shooting at us as well.

Happily, we all had rather helpful recognition scarves of a bright orangey colour, so we waved these over the side of the Bren carrier as fast as we could, and they stopped firing.

You would not believe how enraged the kilted and red-faced company commander was when we got up to them, I think they were the Argylls, saying: "What the bloody hell do you think you're doing? You're damn lucky we didn't blow you to bits."

I received a right old rocket. Of course, I had to apologise. I didn't half feel a fool. I couldn't very well say we'd made a cock-up with the map-reading, but I should have realised we were in a bit of a pickle before we'd got to the crossroads in St Martin des Besaces. In spite of all that it was quite a successful OP but, I tell you what, getting there was one of the hairiest experiences of the war for me.

THE QUESTION OF FEAR

Someone once asked me: "What about fear?"

Well, of course, anyone who says he was never afraid is an idiot. Because we were all quite terrified at times. But I think I have a rather slow reaction, metabolism or something, so I didn't suddenly react with fear, somehow. I know that where I did have one or two sticky spots, I had a funny sort of creepy feeling in my head, it's difficult to describe. It may seem rather strange but I've always believed in guardian angels and, as Mother died when I was 13, I've always felt that she was keeping an eye on me, wherever she was. And wherever there was a particularly nasty situation, somehow, if I had this creepy feeling on my head, I felt things would be all right. Fortunately, they did turn out okay.

Going back to fear: I think the time I was most put out, most frightened, really, was not actually during the fighting itself, because then I think your adrenaline gets you all keyed up and excited and you're prepared to put up with most things when you're actually in action. But this was at a demonstration showing the power of artillery fire. I can't remember exactly where it was, but somewhere in the Thetford Chase area. There was a viewing stand and about 100 officers were sitting in this stand under a canvas shelter in case it rained. We were looking down over a forward slope, watching shells bursting in the distant target area on the various targets. All of a sudden there was a bang just near us, and two officers sitting only the length of a dining table away from me, just collapsed with blood pouring out of their necks.

Apparently what had happened was that a shell had burst just behind this canvas cover and, of course, canvas will stop nothing. The fragments had gone through and shattered arteries in their necks. Then they turned a peculiar yellowy grey colour and were dead within minutes. It was quite frightening for the rest of us, because the artillery demonstration shoot didn't stop. All the time we were wondering what was going to happen next. That is an example of where fear can suddenly appear when you're not keyed up, and you're expecting to be sitting in relative peace and quiet. It's quite different when you're in the thick of it and expecting to be in trouble.

AUGUST 1944 – MORE LIAISON DUTIES

After the OP at St Martin des Besaces, I had one or two special liaison officer jobs to do because our regiment was moved as part of the AGRA's varying roles in support. Several regiments of the AGRA were sent to support different brigades or divisions, or whatever, depending on the need. Up till then we'd been supporting the 15th (Scottish) Division.

By this time we were getting towards the right flank of the British Army where it was linking up with the Americans. The division to our right was the 11th Armoured Division, so we were moved further over, to the south, to back the 3rd British Division instead of the 15th (Scottish) Division.

That meant there were many new people to meet and get to know. One of my functions there was to meet the various brigade HQs of the 3rd Division, get to know their people and let them know what support we were able to give from the AGRA. I was able to do this from the experience I'd had in the exercises, and when I'd controlled various AGRA shoots, I had a pretty good idea what we could do. My first contact with them was after we'd got down to Vire, round about 9 or 10 August when I got back to the battery from these liaison jobs.

THE 'POCKET PISTOL' SHOOTS

Things were beginning to hot up and we were getting to move a bit further. After the break-up of the German tanks when they'd tried to attack earlier and made a mess of it, we started to feel the jaws were eventually going to close.

We didn't realise yet just how much of a mess the enemy were in. They were really backed into a corner. What had in part led to that was that all the river bridges had been smashed by the RAF's bombing. The Air Force had done a wonderful job. The enemy couldn't bring up ammunition and supplies, they couldn't bring up stores, they couldn't get reinforcements. They did jolly well, actually. For all that, they were a pretty competent army. But the destruction caused by the bombing was really far more than they'd bargained for and a great help to us.

At Vire, Archie Campbell our brigadier had the idea of using our battery as what he called his 'pocket pistol'. Our American Long Tom 155mm guns had a range of 27,000 yards (24,700m), about 17 miles (27km). The idea was to move our battery right up with the leading infantry and have us shoot at maximum range. Some of the shoots were done in concert with RAF fighter planes that worked with us through an RAF liaison officer. It was rather like our own air OP, but flying much higher so they could go with more safety over the German lines, controlling our fire at this maximum range.

The Germans had no idea we could reach such a great distance ahead. With our shells striking far further than they expected, they were persuaded to think we were much further advanced than we actually were. Archie Campbell began to use us as his pocket pistol when our battery had been brought up to Vire to fire far forward at maximum range. I then had an AGRA OP job as my turn came round once my liaison jobs had finished. The liaison business was itself quite tricky, not knowing exactly who was where. There was no continuous front line. Probably quite frequently I went into gaps where neither side was in control. Either way, I had to go on and my job then was to go forward and see what support we could give as an AGRA to the 3rd British Division.

Our road went south-east from Vire, and we eventually caught up with 3 Division's recce regiment, The Royal Northumberland Fusiliers, at Tinchebray. I found them there in a little orchard on the left of the main road. Tinchebray was a small pretty town, about the same size as Clare, near us in Suffolk. With the town behind us the orchard was near a fork in the road, and the fork to the right headed towards Flers. (image 18)

Along the Flers road they'd had a couple of armoured scout cars that had hit mines, been blown up, and were a bit of a mess. Nothing could be driven past for some time. As we approached the recce squadron, the Germans started shelling this main street we were on. There were quite a lot of the squadron's vehicles along the road, and it was pretty obvious that the enemy had got observation of the road from somewhere.

We turned round on a sixpence, as fast as you can imagine, and belted further back down the road to get out of sight. I went back on foot to find the commander of this squadron of the recce regiment. When I'd made myself known to him, he said: "I reckon the Germans must have an OP from the tower of Frênes church you can see over there. If you can knock that down or do some serious damage to it, that would be terrific."

So off we went. It was pretty difficult because we didn't know who was where. The enemy could see us but we couldn't see where they were, apart from that church tower. At that moment none of our chaps was getting any further than that fork in the road at Tinchebray, so our British spearhead was being held back. (image 21)

However, on the map I could see there was a farm track, which proved to be not much of a track, going up to the north and east of Tinchebray. I thought maybe we could wangle ourselves round and get somewhere with a view of this church at Frênes so that we could direct a shoot onto it. It was all pretty scary because the farm track was typical of the Bocage, narrow with high hedges along each side and nowhere to turn round. We didn't know who was in front, we didn't know if the track was mined.

Driving slowly, we drew to a halt beside an old farmhouse, and I thought we'd just see if there was anyone there who could tell us about the Germans' positions. So I went in and there was the poor farmer lying dead in his hallway. The place was deserted and smashed up, so the Germans had obviously been and gone. There was no sign of them. That was quite upsetting.

Eventually we managed to get further round, and at last I managed to get a very good view of this church at Frênes from a lightly concealed spot behind a hedge. (image 22)

We managed to get fire down, pretty hefty fire, on their OP. Sven and I had a bit of a snag here in that we were in the direct line from the guns to the target. We were shooting just a bit south-east from Vire and the range was between 9,000 and 10,000 yards, something like 5 miles. This wasn't much for us as we could shoot up to 17 miles, but the precarious thing about this was we were in the hundred per cent zone.

This was a fairly small cigar-shaped area into which all the shells should land. We had crept forward from the Bren carrier with the remote control to the spot where we could see the church tower but hopefully could not be seen from it. Sven and I were crouched in the shade of a hedge, but we were towards the bottom end of the hundred per cent zone.

We had to risk the chance that one of our shells might land at the bottom end of the hundred per cent zone where we were. We had to trust to luck and to the accuracy of our guns, our battery were very good, Jack Tremlett, our gun position officer, was excellent and very accurate. They really knew what they were doing. We hoped. So we did a controlled shoot and made a substantial mess of the German OP in the church, but, thank goodness, not of ourselves.

When we got back safely into Tinchebray, the squadron commander said: "Well, that's certainly shut them up and made a terrific difference, thank god. Now maybe we can get on with our job and they can't."

Having said that, he didn't really want to go further that evening. He suggested that if we could get some supporting fire down during the night, that would be really helpful and should prevent the enemy from organising themselves to attack us there in Tinchebray again. To do this we needed to shell around the area of Frênes, beyond it round another village called Montsecret just north of Frênes and a couple of miles to the east.

I told him the only way to guarantee to do that would be to go back to the regiment and show the commanding officer on the map just exactly what was where, and to lay on various timed shoots during the night. Of course, I explained, they wouldn't be observed, but at least it would be regular shooting. So I said: "If you'll just show me exactly where you want us to shoot, I'll go and clear it with them and point the guns in the right direction."

It was dark by then, so we had a fairly nightmarish ride back to RHQ. When we got there I saw Colonel Roderick MacLeod and brought him up to scratch on the details. He then laid it on with all the batteries, and they kept up pretty constant shooting during the night. We didn't sleep, of course, and we got back to the 3rd British Division's recce regiment before dawn, and made contact again.

The commanding officer said that that the nicest thing overnight was a sort of slipping sound as our shells came overhead. It seemed to him that they had fallen just where they were wanted, so that had been pretty effective.

When I got back to the regiment and laid on this shoot overnight with the commanding officer, Colonel MacLeod said: "Now you've made the contact with this 3 Division recce regiment, we don't want to send up someone else who doesn't know the form or what's going on up there. You've worked with them and shown them what we can do, so they trust you to do the job and, hopefully, you're going to do them some good. You'd better stay with them for the next twenty-four hours."

That meant we wouldn't get much sleep, but back we went to Tinchebray.

TINCHEBRAY TO LANDISACQ

When dawn came, we breakfasted early. By that time they'd shifted their damaged scout cars where the mines were during the night, and we moved on gradually along the road to a little village called Landisacq. That was quite a way along, possibly two-thirds of the way to Flers.

There'd been one or two exchanges of machine-gunfire, but we pressed on. Our good old Bren gun carrier went along behind a couple of the leading scout cars, and we had a Jeep following along behind. We stopped for a moment or two when Captain Alexander, who was leading the patrol, came along and said:

> I think what we'd better do now is this. You and I can go on slightly ahead in my Jeep. We can get out of any trouble pretty quickly and we're less likely to trigger any mines. We can have a look and see what's happening up ahead. It seems to me there's not very much left here. I think the Germans have been a bit put out by your guns firing so far ahead, and have pulled back a bit. So, tell you what, just the two of us can edge forward and get the gen on the situation further up the road.

He handed me an American Winchester rifle, a weapon I'd never fired and never did. I had my own pistol at my side as well, of course. I'm pretty sure once Captain Alexander and I had begun to move forward ahead of the recce patrol scout cars, it is very likely our Jeep was the very first Allied vehicle at the tip of the advance across Normandy, the very point of the spear.

LANDISACQ TO FLERS: OUT OF A DITCH

So, we tootled along this main road from Landisacq towards Flers. When we'd gone a mile or so from the edge of Flers, just as we were going round the bend all of a sudden, out of the ditch, leapt a rather smartly dressed French chap, dark-haired and dressed in riding breeches and a blazer with a Royalist badge on the pocket. (image 23)

I nearly shot him.

We stopped, and between his broken English and our broken French he claimed that a lot of the Germans had retreated out of Flers, although there were still some around. He told us he had been able to ride round Flers on his bike earlier because the Germans were used to seeing him, he had noted many of their defensive positions, and he could show us where they were.

"I can even mark them on your map for you, if you like."

We didn't really know whether to trust him or not but we thought we'd take a gamble on it, so we did. It soon transpired his name was Robert Duguey, and we became good friends as time went by. (images 24 and 25)

However, we thought we'd better first go back and tell the squadron what we were going to do. They came up very carefully behind us.

We took Robert Duguey with us and when we'd briefed them, Alexander got into his scout car with Duguey and I went with Sven and my other chaps, and we drove on into Flers, the first British soldiers to enter the city.

We left our vehicles somewhere in the middle of the town where, as far as I could see, all the roads seemed to meet, and tentatively went forward on foot.

It was an amazing, taut feeling.

We could see a great many open windows where hidden snipers could shoot from.

Then all of a sudden, round a corner came a funny looking German Kubelwagen jalopy, a couple of cooks aboard with dixies full of coffee. We stopped them and took them prisoner, and put their vehicle on one side.

Naturally we commandeered that vehicle, and the coffee, for the battery and after this operation we eventually took it with us into Holland. But that's another story.

17. *The fold in the landscape where about sixty enemy tanks were assembled near the hedge and trees in the middle distance, taken in 1994 more or less from an observation point 300 or 400 yards away from the target (Jes Mainwaring)*

18. *Looking down the road to Flers from Tinchebray from the orchard where the Recce Squadron was forced to halt. Taken in 1994 (Jes Mainwaring)*

19. *The crossroads at St Martin des Besaces some while later. Motorised infantry of the 8th Rifle Brigade advancing under the protection of tanks of the 23rd Hussars (I.W.M. B 8292)*

20. *The same crossroads at St Martin des Besaces in 1994, fifty years later (Jes Mainwaring)*

21. *The tower of Frênes church concealing the German artillery; OP, just visible on the upper left. Taken from the fork in the road in 1994 (Jes Mainwaring)*

22. *Frênes church tower, which hid the German OP, in 1994. The 'very good view from our lightly concealed spot.' (Jes Mainwaring)*

23. Our approach road to Flers where Robert jumped out of the ditch. The track leads to the Duguey cottage. Photo taken 1994 (Jes Mainwaring)

24. Robert Duguey briefing the squadron on enemy positions around Flers, 15 August 1944 (Restaged later for British Army Film Unit) (I.W.M B 9297)

25. *Robert Duguey showing German defensive positions to Harry on a map. Near Flers, 15 August 1944 (Restaged later for British Army Film Unit) (I.W.M B 9298)*

26. *Robert's younger brother Gaetan takes Harry back to the same cemetery back gate where Robert had led them in 1944, photographed in 1994 (Jes Mainwaring)*

27. The hidden path through the cemetery where Harry and his companions made their unseen approach to attack the anti-tank gun position (Jes Mainwaring)

28. The anti-tank gun was positioned in the middle of the road. The unguarded gateway can be seen in the cemetery wall beyond (Jes Mainwaring)

29. *Checking the way ahead for mines in the main street of Flers after the arrival of 11th Armoured Division (I.W.M B 9290)*

Above: **30.** *The Dugueys' cottage near Flers in 1994 (Jes Mainwaring)*

Left: **31.** *M. Duguey Snr and Anne-Marie at the door of their cottage*

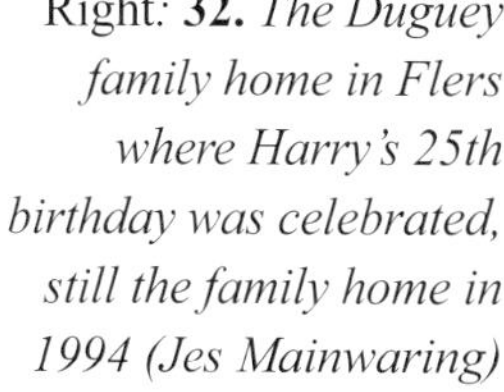

Right: **32.** *The Duguey family home in Flers where Harry's 25th birthday was celebrated, still the family home in 1994 (Jes Mainwaring)*

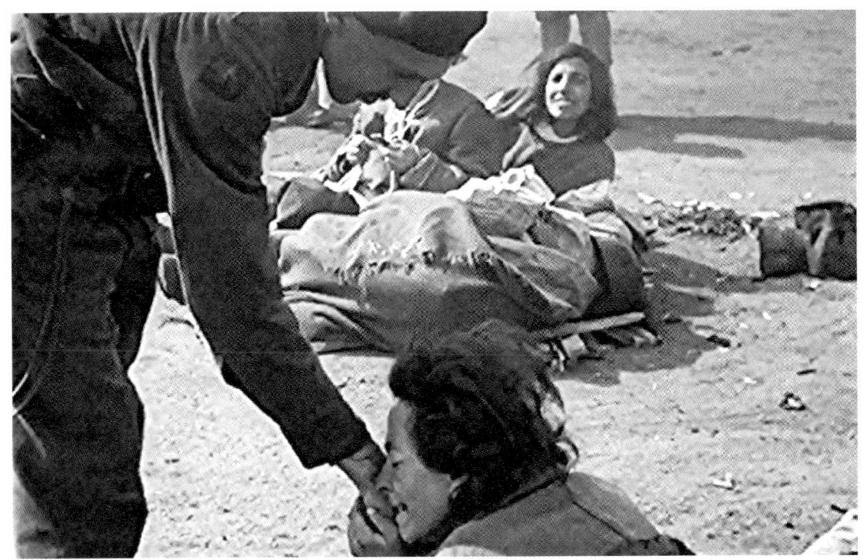

33. A British soldier in Belsen, unequivocally believed by Harry and his family to be Harry. Unlike his shoulder flash his distinctive profile is clear, and he remembers noticing a cameraman filming him in that place. When this film clip was first shown publicly in the TV series World at War, *the unexpected recollection caused Harry considerable distress as, like many other British soldiers who witnessed that terrible place, he had suppressed the memory. Over the telephone his voice cracked. "I just saw myself in Belsen."*

This clip has since been included in many feature and documentary films and has become an iconic expression of human compassion.

The film is in the care of the Imperial War Museum, who maintain the soldier is a cameraman with the film unit. He appears to be wearing a lanyard leading to a leather revolver holster with a brass stud, very similar to the holster Harry wore throughout the war, previously used by his father in the First World War. In a sense his identity does not matter, as he represents every British soldier who risked all in the liberation of Europe. (IWM FLM1226)

34. *The last parade*

15 AUGUST 1944 – THE LIBERATION OF FLERS

After that refreshing but unexpected excitement, we cautiously carried on with our recce along the main road out from the town centre, which ominously lead to the cemetery. This led up a gentle gradient and we reached a bit of a crest on the hill, with the straight road running behind us back to the town centre.

"LOOK OUT!" Sven yelled suddenly.

In the distance way up the road was a bright sharp flash. *BANG!* And an enemy shell crashed against the building right beside us. The enemy clearly had an anti-tank gun up the road. Sven, who had a familiar British rifle, quick as lightning put it to his shoulder and opened up with a shot or two straight at those chaps.

This was not good.

"Bloody hell. We'd better do something about this," we decided with little hesitation.

By now we'd distinctly got the feeling that Robert Duguey had been telling us the truth about the Germans there. Robert told us he knew a discreet way through the back alleys that would lead into the lower part of the cemetery. (image 26)

I made sure Robert was unarmed because I didn't want the Germans to take it out on his family if the plan went off the rails. With Robert as our guide, Sven, Captain Alexander, Blanchard and I went back on ourselves, slightly downhill and out of sight of the anti-tank gunners.

We crossed the road, entered the cemetery and, clutching our weapons, managed to creep very quietly back up the hill, concealed behind the 7- or 8-foot high cemetery wall. (image 27)

Finally, level with the anti-tank gun in the middle of the road, 20 or 30 yards away, was an open unguarded gateway through the cemetery wall. The element of surprise was firmly on our side as we rushed the gun from the gateway, firing as we attacked. (image 28)

We shot them up pretty thoroughly, and managed to put the gun crew out of action.

I suppose it was a pretty exciting business really, the sort that makes you feel lucky to be alive. I had started out in this war leaving behind my studies along with the intention of taking Holy Orders, to confront the face of the unforgiveable.

It was the experience of close contact actions like this that left me feeling I was no longer able to pursue such a high calling. As Robert's younger brother Gaetan recalled later when remembering his brother Robert's description of the action, being outnumbered we were in no position to take prisoners. It was partly due to this action I was subsequently greatly honoured to be awarded the Military Cross.

Robert had marked the Germans' outlying positions around Flers on my map. This action had made clear that discretion is probably the better part of valour, so I reckoned we'd better get this information back to the regiment so the enemy positions could be properly shot up. That night heavy fire was directed onto the targets identified on the map and by morning there was no further resistance.

That really was our main job there done. We'd gone through Tinchebray, we'd laid down heavy fire between Tinchebray and Landisacq, and we'd gone on to Flers. I suppose we considered we'd liberated Flers by then because we knew there was no longer much sign of the enemy about the place.

The following day, the 11th Armoured Division came in and mopped up, although I don't think there was all that much mopping-up to be done. Most of the enemy had vanished, and we'd cleared the only people showing any activity when we took out that anti-tank gun. It had clearly been performing a rearguard action, protecting the Germans' escape road into the Falaise pocket. (image 29)

With that action over, we headed back to the battery. Now that we trusted him, we took Robert with us to drop him off at his family's cottage outside the town where they had been living for the time being. On the way, he said: "Why don't you call in now on your way back, and meet my family?"

We were delighted to accept. It was a much appreciated break and extreme change of scene for us. They made us very welcome. A reminder of why we were fighting.

They were overjoyed that liberation had come at last.

We met Robert's whole family. His father and mother, his three sisters and younger brother Gaetan. Anne-Marie and Gaetan were the two youngest at around 10 or 11. Madeleine was about 19 and came to stay with us in Cambridge after the war. The oldest was Odile, a rather quiet girl who later became a nun. (image 31)

20 AUGUST 1944 – TWENTY-FIFTH BIRTHDAY PARTY

We continued our journey back to the battery to find the regiment had been taken out of the line and held back for a few days. A couple of days after we'd returned on 18 August, I managed to scrounge a vehicle and Sven and I went over to see the Dugueys at their cottage near Flers. (image 30)

It came out in conversation that my twenty-fifth birthday was due on the twentieth. On hearing this Madame Duguey said: "*Eh bien*, 'Arry, you must bring all your officers and we will give you a magnificent birthday party."

In due course, on the twentieth, we all, except one who was left behind as duty officer at the battery, turned up at their rather grand town house in Flers. There we were, all ready for a birthday party in the middle of the chaos of war. They'd baked me a birthday cake, heaven knows what the ingredients were or where they got them from. They'd even managed to ice it. However Madame Duguey achieved it, it tasted delightful, I can tell you.

They produced champagne, which they dug up out of the garden where they had hidden it when the Germans occupied their area. They'd made wax candles for the cake. God knows where they got the wax, but they'd done it. It was a super spread, it really was as magnificent as promised.

Many years later, in 1961, Sven Berlin's first book was published by Gollancz, entitled *I am Lazarus*. Whilst claiming not to be an autobiography, the book tells Sven's view of the war from his eyes, those of a poet and artist. It may have been in anticipation of returning to his artists' community in Cornwall, or the demands of his own self-perception in later life as a former conscientious objector that led Sven to almost brush out the close-contact intensity of the anti-tank gun incident in Flers.

These first months in Normandy feature extensively in Sven's book, where I have the privilege of being referred to simply as 'the captain'. Of our meetings with the Dugueys, Sven writes:

I thought I saw Robert sigh and look across at Madeleine. It was understandable: they were young. Myself and the Captain: were we not soldiers from another country, fighting, bringing our gifts and customs – we also were still young men, poet and priest in spirit and intention, if not truly worthy of such sacred denominations. For them there must have been romance in our coming; we held their future. What will Anne-Marie say when she grows up?

'I remember English soldiers coming to our house after the city had fallen to the British. I was twelve.

They talked of poetry and religion and of England, but not of war. It is clear to me now, the memory of them sitting in the dining-room at home. They were both quite young men. Their uniforms were strange to me after the grey uniforms of the Germans and they seemed easy together even though they were of different rank. So different to our French household; and their language was strange because we hadn't been taught English at school while the Germans were in occupation. When they tried to speak French it was very funny. We had had a hard time with the Germans. I did not fully understand what it meant to be free; my childhood had saved me from a good deal. I did not know what growing up in the new world would mean. Happily I was young enough to forget the bombs, the great fire, the rifle shots in the streets. They went away – these two – in an army truck. It was dark. I thought of them chasing the Germans out of France. The taste of chocolate and the scent and feel of soap were the texture of my new world, woven with the laughter of these men and the look on their faces when they talked of their homes…'

After the party we went back to the battery. During one of my liaison jobs I'd met and become quite friendly with a chap who was an air OP pilot, flying a little Auster spotter plane. Two or three days after the party I met him again, told him about it, and asked: "Do you think you could do me a bit of a favour, and take me on a little flight over Flers in your Auster so I could drop a message of thanks to the Dugueys?"

"Certainly, of course," he said. "Good idea, be a nice little trip."

So up we went in his little Auster. I had a message pouch, and put a letter of thanks in it in my best but not very good French, and a small framed Mainwaring family coat of arms drawn by my father. I tied a lovely silk streamer onto the pouch and we flew low over their house.

Madeleine and her mother came out to see what was going on. When they realised that someone was waving directly at them, I dropped the message pouch with its streamer trailing behind. They rushed over to retrieve it and waved their thanks and off we flew, back to the landing field.

In 1994 I went back to Normandy for the fiftieth anniversary celebrations with my younger son Jes and family. I met up with Anne-Marie and Gaetan again, who by 1994 were in their early 60s and still living at their family home in Flers. Incredibly, Anne-Marie still had the stubs of the candles, which she had made herself aged 12, from my twenty-fifth birthday cake. Anne-Marie invited us into their home, and in the dining room pointed out exactly where each one of us sat, by name, round their dining table at my party fifty years earlier. (image 32)

Later during my visit I was proud to be made a Freeman of Flers at a civic ceremony in the town hall, after which Anne-Marie and Gaetan entertained us all to a celebratory lunch. Sadly the person missing from that celebration who I would have dearly loved to have been with us at the table was Robert himself. He had passed away three years earlier.

During my visit we went to stay with Madeleine, who had married Pierre Tarwé, a Belgian, in Tournai. On 20 August they gave me a seventy-fifth birthday dinner, fifty years to the day after they celebrated my twenty-fifth in Flers at the height of the war and the moment of their liberation. During dinner Madeleine produced from an elegant antique cabinet my father's meticulously drawn

Mainwaring coat of arms, which I had dropped with my message from the Auster in 1944.

It is strange and worth the occasional comment how years afterwards people you have known, often in intense times, come back however briefly into your life. The world truly is a small place.

When I was an assistant district commissioner with the Boy Scouts in Cambridge, I went out to the RAF station at Waterbeach. We were laying on something there for the Scouts to do a brief course for the weatherman badge, and I was introduced to the meteorological officer at the RAF station.

Unbelievably, he transpired to be Captain Alexander, with whom I made that tentative spearpoint advance into unknown territory, where we met Robert and entered Flers. He had left his regiment at the end of the war and gone as a civilian into the meteorological service. All RAF stations have a permanent meteorological officer, and here it was Captain Alexander, stationed at Waterbeach. Needless to say, we had a very pleasant few minutes discussing the events we'd shared in 1944.

THE FALAISE GAP CLOSES

Going back to 1944, after Flers we were happy to be out of the line for a bit of rest and recuperation. The Allied pincers had closed with the Battle of the Falaise Gap by 20 August and trapped the remaining Germans who hadn't been able to escape further east. The Falaise Pocket had been sealed on the very day we were having my birthday party in Flers, so it seems we had another reason to celebrate.

Of course, news travels quickly. We knew we'd got most of them in the bag, so Peter Selfe and I got into Peter's Jeep and swanned off, looking around to see just what chaos looked like. It was almost unbelievable. Dust and rubble. There were dead bodies everywhere, people, animals, more dust. There were smashed vehicles. There was an incredible number of horse-drawn wagons, which we just hadn't expected to see.

Our armies were entirely mechanised, and we hadn't realised how much of the German second line transport was horse-drawn. It was quite a revelation to us.

By about 28 August, the River Seine, which is a pretty wide river, had been crossed at Vernon. Vernon had been captured after a sticky battle by the 43rd (Wessex) Division. Their engineers had managed to get a couple of bridges across the river, a heavy one for tanks and a lighter one for smaller vehicles, so we were able to continue our advance further east.

The RAF had done a terrific job of smashing the original bridges, which prevented the Germans from getting the reinforcements they'd hoped for to help them beat us back. But, of course, it was now difficult for us in our turn as we tried to advance to the east because we then had to build new bridges to replace those that were destroyed.

SEPTEMBER 1944 – MOVING EAST

It was early September when we began to move eastwards again. It must have been about 140 miles to Vernon from where we were near Vire, where our guns had remained whilst we were swanning around in Flers. We eventually crossed over the Seine at Vernon and laagered somewhere just to the east of there for a time.

We were beginning to advance more quickly now that we'd crossed the Seine to go east to Paris, as well as to the north and south of Paris. To help the supply situation, units like ours who had been in action continually and were supposed to be rested had to lose their load-carrying trucks. The trucks with their drivers, who got no rest, were needed for temporary duties to make up the convoys taking stores, ammunition and so on up to the troops who were now furthest forward.

Elsewhere, clearing Antwerp was proving to be a slow and very nasty job and it still hadn't been captured. The River Scheldt is the main access to the port of Antwerp, which is quite a long way inland from the sea, and that hadn't been cleared either. All the stores were still coming over the beaches at Arromanches, and our vehicles were diverted to support the troops who were dashing forward.

The Germans were completely broken after the Falaise Gap, and they were going back as quickly as possible towards the Rhine to get back to the borders of Germany, leaving various pockets of resistance in the coastal ports. They kept, for example, the garrisons at Boulogne and Calais.

The Guards Armoured Division dashed on and liberated Brussels to great rejoicing. For understandable emotional and political reasons, de Gaulle's Free French went in to liberate Paris. Whilst that was going on, our regiment, having crossed the Seine, was diverted to the west coast, moving up towards Boulogne and Calais.

MUSHROOMS IN BEAUVAIS

On our way there we stopped for a short time in Beauvais, north-west of Paris. Beauvais had already been liberated by the Guards Division, who'd then rushed on to Brussels. There we danced in the square to the jigging of the old-fashioned French accordions I'd only heard before on scratchy gramophone records.

Whilst we were there one of my friends I'd met on some of my liaison trips, Gleb Kerensky, turned up. He was a captain in the REME, and his father had been the last post-revolutionary interim government prime minister of Russia before the Bolsheviks finally took over.

Gleb and his mother had been forced to flee for months through the Russian forests to get away from the Bolsheviks and eventually they reached Paris. I'd heard a number of his extraordinary tales of their journey for survival, and necessity had caused them to learn an awful lot about edible fungi. He went on to say: "Here's an idea. The forest around Beauvais here will be full of them, so why don't we go and forage for some fungi and I'll cook us a meal like nothing you've ever had."

With my heart in my mouth and a lingering suspicion of all those fungi, we went mushroom-hunting. He obviously knew his way around fungi, picking out the safe ones, and we had an amazing meal. I was expecting to drop dead of poisoning any minute, but I'm still here so it must have been all right.

PREMONITION AT BOULOGNE

From Beauvais we went north-west right to the coast, attacking Boulogne first. The important thing here, and the main reason the Germans wanted to hold on to it, was that Boulogne was a big German 'E-boat' base, their fast torpedo boats. On top of this it was also a major position for launching sites for the 'buzz bomb', the V1 'doodlebug' flying bomb, directly across the English Channel, bringing London and elsewhere within range. Early in September our heavy guns bombarded Boulogne. Sadly, but inevitably, this compounded the effects of the aerial bombing its people had already suffered, but also broke the Nazi occupation forces enough to enable the Canadians to retake and finally liberate the town.

One evening, while we were at Boulogne, I had a most awful headache, absolutely ghastly. I've never had a headache like it before or since. I found myself feeling, out of the blue, suddenly very concerned about my wife Peggy and if she was all right.

> *Peggy:*
> *Part of our daily lives were the V1 'doodlebug' flying bombs. If you looked out of the kitchen window in the Black Cottage, there were two trees. You knew that if a doodlebug came between those trees it came straight over the house. This particular time I could hear this pom-pom-pom noise like a motorbike. I looked out of the window and saw it coming straight towards us. It was coming towards us but it was very low, and suddenly the engine seemed to stop and you knew it was going to crash. It went over, it must have just scraped between the two big old chimneys on the Black Cottage. Of course I was upstairs, terrified – I rushed over to Simon in the cot – there was nothing I could do – I remember thinking I suppose this is it, but the motor must have started up again and it continued flying. The room was full of sulphur-smelling exhaust fumes, it was absolutely awful. The doodlebug crashed into the side of Danbury Hill where the hill rose out of the landscape about a mile away. It went straight into a cottage and killed two old ladies in their 80s who lived there.*

It transpired from our letters that on that very day and at the same time I'd had this awful headache, almost unbelievably Peggy had had the most terrifying experience at the Black Cottage with Simon. One of those doodlebugs had gone right over the Black Cottage between the two chimneys. There was Peggy, frozen with fear and holding baby Simon as this flying bomb went overhead sounding like a motorbike, so very close to their home. It crashed and blew up on a hillside only a short distance away. I believe in some way Peggy's absolute terror communicated itself to me –

more things in heaven and on earth than are ever dreamt of, I suppose.

After we'd finished at Boulogne we went on to bombard Calais. Calais was the main base for the German radar that was tracking our convoys through the English Channel. So it was absolutely vital that we dealt with it. We supported the Canadians' attack on 17 September when they used flail tanks, which they'd used earlier in Normandy. On the same day the RAF's heavy bombers also attacked Calais rather like they'd done at Caen but with greater precision.

Calais didn't surrender until 1 October. But in the meantime, we had to dash off to support the Arnhem landings.

HOLLAND AND BELGIUM

With these jobs over, the regiment moved to the east to mingle with the armour on the Belgian/Dutch border. On our way, I remember going through many of the places whose names I'd often heard my father talking about from the First World War: St Omer; Haazebrook; Armentières, where the 'mademoiselle, parley voo' came from; and a whole lot of the famous places the books and songs of the First World War mentioned. Eventually, we went on through Tournai, where Madeleine Duguey now lives, and up across just south of the site of the Battle of Waterloo to Louvain. And then we went on into Holland.

We just about got up to Eindhoven. Time was going by and there was this great idea of Monty's of swooping round and breaking through with the Allies crossing the Rhine and swanning across the north German plain. Of course, the story about all that is well known now. There was only one main road joining Nijmegen to Arnhem, and the British 2nd Army couldn't get through to relieve the Paras at Arnhem.

We went on *post-haste* after we'd got into Holland, up through Helmond and Gennep, and then eventually we reached Nijmegen. We had our guns in a school playing field behind a row of semi-detached houses, and we were firing as much as we could at the known German positions in Arnhem. The people who lived in those semi-detached houses, whose lives had been taken over by years of brutal occupation and whose windows were now being shattered by the shockwaves from our gunfire, brought us welcome cups of tea.

Sadly, it didn't do much good. It was quite a time before any British troops were able to get through to Arnhem once the airborne force remnants had been withdrawn across the river or captured. I have a family connection here. My cousin Joan's husband, and my close friend, Captain Foster Robson MC, was a glider pilot and landed well outside Arnhem as planned. He eventually got into Arnhem and was wounded there and eventually taken prisoner.

It was so sad that so many men were killed or wounded or taken prisoner, but it was an extraordinarily brave effort. The weather, especially a spell of thick fog, and various other things conspired against it. It just didn't come off, it was famously that 'bridge too far'.

After as many of the Arnhem forces who could get out across the river were withdrawn, we were sent quite a bit south-ish from Nijmegen, and on to Helmond and Deurne. These places were liberated a few days after the airborne forces had been brought back from Arnhem.

At Deurne, Dr Johnny Clark, who was our family doctor all the time we were in Fen Ditton after the war, was a regimental medical officer. He earned a very well-deserved MC at Deurne for insisting on rescuing men from a burning tank that was under fire. His was probably one of the best deserved MCs of that time in the war. A very brave man.

After that, we headed south and east, because there was a substantial pocket of Germans still south-west of the Rhine, still in Holland. We had a gun position at Asten and the Americans' boundary, with whom we had a friendly rivalry, was somewhere near there. I recall a pretty sticky situation before we got there where some of the Scottish chaps lived up to their fighting history.

There was a famous American division nearby, the 7th Cavalry I believe. But the Germans broke through. One of the Scottish brigades was sent in to stop their advance, which they achieved with overwhelming success. The Germans then had no choice but to retreat further east.

TRAGEDY AT ASTEN

A very sad thing that shouldn't have happened occurred at our gun position in Asten. It was rather sandy soil there and the gun position chaps had dug pits beside the guns, roofed them over and had got little fires going down there to keep themselves warm.

The gun position NCOs should have been in tighter control and put a stop to how they were achieving this. We had no idea that the gun detachments had taken small bags of cordite down into these gun pits. After a time, there was a tendency to become overconfident around the guns.

As described above, various charges were made up of bags of cordite. The more bags used, the greater the range of the shell. When you were firing at shorter ranges, there were bags left over and the men were making the small fires down in their bunkers burn more brightly by adding little bits of cordite to them.

They were storing these bags of cordite under the benches they'd made down there. One day the inevitable happened. The temperature in one of the dugouts got beyond the flash point of cordite and, *WHOOSH!* up those bags of cordite went, and about twelve chaps staggered out of this dugout, burned, terribly burned. For the first time we saw the new use of salt water as first aid treatment on burns.

They were taken away as quickly as possible to the field hospital, skin coming off all over them, terrible blisters. They never came back to us. It should never have happened, and was one of those occasions that proves that stupidly ignoring basic rules of safety, with ammunition or anything else, can really lead to terrible consequences. A ghastly business.

Peggy:
Hoffmans in Chelmsford was a factory where they made ball-bearings and things twenty-four hours a day, essential for arms production. There were storage tanks in the roof above the top floor holding large amounts of paraffin, which dripped in a gentle 'rain' of paraffin down along the wall from above. The girls used this to wash the machine oil off the steel balls for the bearings.

One night without warning one of those new V2 rockets fell next to Hoffmans. The flashover set fire to the paraffin and it was like a waterfall of fire all the way down that wall and all those girls were burnt to death, about two hundred of them were killed. I remember Emily's husband Bill, who was working at Hoffmans too, along with Emily. He helped to get them out. They went through the wreckage to get them. Some of those poor girls' bodies were shrunk to the size of dogs.

Jes (2022):

I grew up having heard this terrible story as a child, but it does have a kind of healing sequel. Fifty years after this tragic event I was able in a way, as an architect, to 'square the circle'. The old Hoffmans factory site had become redundant, the old abandoned buildings were mostly demolished, and the site was acquired by Anglia Ruskin University as the home for their new Chelmsford campus. As a new university their aim was a high level of education for an international student body, and knowledge is an antidote that can undermine the ignorance that leads to conflict. It can breed an understanding that transcends borders. We were appointed to design the university's learning resource centre, the first building on the new campus site, a new type of building combining library and IT hub, faculty centres, lecture theatres, social services, etc. The heart of the new university.

For this project we were awarded from the European Union, now almost without national borders itself, research and

> *development funding to investigate innovative strategies of environmental and low-energy building design within the 'Queens Building'. Happily the project achieved widespread recognition as a Green Building of the Year in 1996. In doing so, on a personal level it fired for me one of the closing rounds of the Second World War. But it also fired an opening round in the new war against climate change that all humanity faces together.*

OCTOBER 1944 – BATTLE OF OVERLOON

Round about this time, following the original plan about overall command, General Eisenhower (Ike) took over command on the ground of all the Allied armies in the field. This meant that Monty reverted to close command of just the 21st Army Group, which was the 2nd British Army and the 1st Canadian Army.

We continued moving up, towards the River Maas. We had a gun position at St Anthonis. There was a big battle at Boxmeer and we were involved with that. Soon after, there was a rather sticky battle at Overloon, which is south of Boxmeer. It's not far from the River Maas and a bit north-west of Venlo.

This battle started on 10 October, but it took three days to capture the village of Overloon. The 1st Suffolks were the main battalion attacking the village. Years afterwards, when I was serving in BAOR (British Army of the Rhine) in the early 1960s, I discovered my great friend Alan Sperling, with whom I was serving in BAOR, had been the adjutant of the 1st Suffolks in that battle at Overloon.

So on Remembrance Sunday, instead of attending the usual parade, we would go together to Overloon, where there is now a beautiful and immaculate British war cemetery, and pay our respects there. Alan and I both had chaps buried there who'd been killed in the Battle of Overloon. It was a very nasty fight, because Overloon was within reach of the German guns of the Siegfried Line. It was a viciously hot spot.

We stopped later for some time in the village at Overloon. The Germans used to do their shelling at particular times so we just used to go to ground at the times we knew they'd be shelling. We were rather more cunning and varied our times for shelling them.

It became a bit static after that. I think it was about a week later that there was another battle in Venray, where there was an important railway junction, which we eventually captured. About a fortnight later we'd managed to get a bridgehead over the River Maas and soon after that a small town called Weert was taken.

Our troops went on a bit further forward whilst we had our guns around Weert itself, and somehow I became friendly with a family there called Kneepkens. We still have a little spoon with a letter 'P' on it which they gave me, saying the 'P' was for Peggy. When I was in Germany again as a regular after the war in 1961, I stayed a night there with them on my way up to join HQ 1 (BR) Corps at Bielefeld. But that is a story for another time.

NEXT STEP: CROSSING THE MAAS

It might help to understand the way the battles were going at this period. If you can imagine that you're looking at a map of that particular area, and then try to visualise a figure from north to south with its legs astride.

Now look at the left leg. That is the River Maas.

The right leg is the River Rhine.

Now the Maas, going down from north to south, passes through Nijmegen, Venlo, Roermond, Maastricht to Liege.

The Rhine, that's the right-hand leg you're looking at, goes from fairly close to Nijmegen on through Wesel, Duisburg, Dusseldorf, Köln (Cologne), and on to Bonn.

Germany, of course, lies to the east of Belgium and Holland, and the border runs just to the east on the right of the River Maas.

The Germans had made an incredible recovery after their disasters in Normandy as they were being pushed back toward their own country. What they were trying to do now was to keep us from getting across the Maas. That river was a major obstacle. They knew that once we'd managed to get across the Maas, the Rhine would be the next.

And after that the end would almost be in sight. The Germans had fought a very good, very hard and very determined battle from the moment we took them by surprise on the D-Day beaches.

Between October and November and on into December, what we were trying to do was to get ourselves, the Allied forces, all lined up with the Americans to our south and the Canadians to the north of us. So the Americans were on our right facing the enemy to the east. We were trying to line up against the River Maas and get as far as we could up to there. We knew we'd got to get across that river and then there was the Rhine to cross. A fairly big, fairly daunting business.

After the battles at Overloon, and Weert after that, we seemed to be generally milling around on demand in the general area between Eindhoven, Venray and Nijmegen. We were called upon to go to this place, and that place, to lay down our particular brand of heavy fire wherever necessary. We went back some time over Christmas to Overloon, which was to be our base for some while.

DECEMBER 1944 – COUNTER-ATTACK

Just before Christmas, there was a sudden and unexpected attack by the Germans, starting on 16 December, from the Ardennes.

In principle, what they were really doing was following their strategy of May 1940, when they'd pushed through the French lines from the Ardennes. This had always been considered to be an area that was not likely to be penetrated easily, if at all.

Idiotically, even with the example of 1940 behind them, the 1944 Allied line in the Ardennes area, which covers most of the tiny country of Luxembourg, was very thinly held by American troops. Some of these were there resting in this lightly defended and relatively 'safe' area fed by fairly thin supply lines. The Germans however, got all their available tanks together and made an overwhelming attack.

They pushed the Americans back, getting through on a front of 40 miles. They went right back, 50 miles into the US lines. There was a famous stand by one of the American divisions, 101st Airborne, at Bastogne. When this sudden attack through the Ardennes and the Germans' breakthrough took place, Eisenhower very quickly gave Field Marshal Montgomery overall command of the north of this salient. This added to Monty's own command of the 21st Army Group consisting of the British and the Canadians, and temporary command of the 1st and the 9th US Armies as well.

On the south side of this bulge, General Omar Bradley was in command. Now bring to mind that picture I painted of the two legs. The left leg was the Belgian and Dutch side going up to Liege, Maastricht and so on. Take Liege as a sort of ankle with the foot turning outwards further to the left, going down to Namur and Charleroi in Belgium. This was where the Germans were aiming.

Their intention was to get right back to Antwerp and split the Allied forces into two. Fortunately, they never actually got as far as the River Maas. It was a phenomenal effort but a fatal mistake for the Germans. They lost almost a quarter of a million men, half of whom were taken as prisoners-of-war, as well as about 1,400 tanks they could ill afford to lose. It was an extremely brave effort, but it was fatal in the end. It just didn't come off for many reasons, and the history books will tell the full story from badly planned logistics to heroic stands, dreadful massacres to the war trials that eventually followed. An appalling part of the conflict.

Although the weather was terrible, the Germans had as many aircraft up as they could when from our battery's point of view an extraordinary thing happened. We were suddenly attacked by one of their planes, and a chap called Murfin, who was one of the sanitary orderlies as well as a first-aid expert, a superb chap and a first class shot with a Bren gun, grabbed his Bren, got the plane in his sights and opened fire. Unbelievably, he actually shot the damned thing down!

As a first-aid man, Murfin had really excelled himself in that ghastly business at Asten when some of the men were badly burned by cordite in their dugout. But this was pretty good. You don't often hear of a plane being shot down by a Bren gunner from the ground. But Murfin managed it, and that was really something special. He got a well-deserved Mention in Dispatches for that.

JANUARY 1945 – THE GREAT THAW

It was a very severe winter. Towards the end of January the Germans' efforts to the south of us had petered out and the Ardennes bulge had been straightened and strengthened again.

The severe winter melted into an incredible thaw.

The roads became absolutely appalling. I've never seen roads break up as they did then. A one-way circuit had to be organised with the traffic making the best of the conditions. Part of the circuit was along a disused railway line, which gave the most bumpy ride. Initially, extra sleepers were put down between the rails. But then the rails themselves had to be taken up and more and more sleepers put down to fill in. It was the most difficult 3 or 4 miles and it didn't do our vehicles much good.

Until the end of January, we continued shooting when the heavy stuff was needed. We remained at Overloon all that time, milling about that circuit around Mill, St Anthonis and back to Overloon.

The Battle of the Reichwald was coming up.

JANUARY INTO FEBRUARY 1945 – PREPARING FOR THE BATTLE OF THE REICHWALD

We had no choice but to get through the Reichwald to advance forward into Germany. In anticipation, there was the biggest programme to create ammunition dumps that we'd had throughout the whole of that north-west European campaign.

I will never forget one sad thing from that time concerning one of our chaps from the wagon lines. The vehicles and support equipment were always kept at a distance from the battery position.

He had some sort of premonition that he was going to be killed. He begged us to relieve him from the job of bringing ammunition up to the gun position itself. But sadly and inevitably everybody who was fit had to go and help to shift the ammunition. And he had to go. Tragically, his premonition came to pass. He was killed when his wagon was blown up as it was being driven up to the gun position.

It was all a very sad business. He was Gunner Horner, and it was to his grave among others in the British War Cemetery that Alan Sperling and I used to go to pay our respects to our dead on Remembrance Sundays in BAOR in the early 1960s.

One of the memories I have almost brings tears to my eyes every time I think of it. When a number of our people, like Gunner Horner, were killed, they had to be buried as quickly as possible. Their graves, with others, were all carefully marked. There were no coffins. Their bodies were left in their battledress uniforms and simply but carefully wrapped in blankets, and they were lowered gently down into their graves.

A particularly heart-rending sight was of their boots, their boots and gaiters dangling on their limp feet, coming out from the blankets around them. Their head, of course, would always be properly covered, but almost always there were their poor feet dangling. It was a very distressing sight, and always upset me very much. The memory still does.

Time went by slowly until the beginning of the Battle of the Reichwald on 8 February. With further stocks of ammunition continually being dumped, we were preparing for, and hoping there would be, a fairly swift breakthrough once we'd got through the Reichwald.

Monty wasn't going to allow the same logistic problems to slow us down this time. No repeat of having to bring all our stores from the Arromanches beach head over 400 miles.

This time there was a massive dumping programme of petrol in 4-gallon Jerrycans all over the place, so that when we did eventually make our breakthrough, the fuel was going to be there. There were special convoys arranged, earmarked in advance, so that we knew a certain number of our vehicles would have to go to help with the dumping programme, bringing fuel up so that whenever there was a swift movement forward, all the proper supplies were available.

8 FEBRUARY 1945 – BATTLE OF THE REICHWALD BEGINS

At last the day was here.

We opened up with a terrific barrage. We fired and fired again and again. All our stock of ammunition we'd had brought up earlier was used up and continually being replaced. I think we fired more in those few days after 8 February whilst the Reichwald was being cleared than we had done anywhere previously. The Reichwald was cleared by 13 February. It took five days of hard slog but we eventually got up to Goch.

It had been a constantly hard road since we'd crossed the Maas at Gennep. Later on, Gennep became the end-station for leave trains to start taking people back to Calais for the Channel crossing back to the UK. Once we'd crossed the Rhine in March, people began to be allowed home leave, with a limited proportion from each unit. There'd been no leave since D-Day in June.

FEBRUARY/MARCH 1945 – THE BANKS OF THE RHINE

For the next four or five weeks after we reached Goch, the aim of the fighting was to try to really consolidate up to the Rhine. It was a continuous slogging battle, pushing the Germans back gradually. Somewhere around the end of the first two weeks of March we'd pushed the Germans back, and forced them right across to the far side of the Rhine.

Then, of course, the next thing for us was to follow this success by getting across the Rhine ourselves. This was a pretty tricky business. Fortunately, the Americans further south managed to get across the Rhine without very much opposition. At our northern end, though, the Germans were reinforcing positions with people digging in to oppose us, and the Canadians to our north.

The Canadians were clearing out the rest of Holland and we were concentrating our forces to get across the Rhine in between Emmerich to the west on the left, with Wesel to the right. They were about 25 miles apart, but it seemed quite a long way in those circumstances.

The chief engineer of 21st Army Group had got the searchlights very cleverly organised so that there was a constant sort of false

How it felt in France. Letter from M. Duguey Snr to Harry's father, 8 May 1945
(Jes Mainwaring)

22 NOV

1994

Dear Harry: "Le recherche du temps perdu!"
And with an artillery barrage of emotion
feeling, clear visual memory, and a
deep stirring in the heart, that was
frightening to get your phone call +
letter with the book & photographs. I
had no idea your friendship with Robert
+ his family was so complete. I think I
sent Lazarus at the time, but that is
all. Since writing it I have had to
put the experience away to be able to
deal with the difficulties + battles of
another kind. I did not take part in
the Remembrance this year, because
only those old men in suits + berets +
medals knew the horror + depth of
suffering + love. They were either
silent or inarticulate + broke down
afterwards. But those who watched
had no idea. I could not have stood
the pressure. I thought Lazarus
had done it for me. Robert Graves,

Letter to Harry from Sven Berlin p1, 1994 (Jes Mainwaring)

when he was advising me about a
tragedy in my own life, looked
very seriously at me when I said:
"It's almost as bad as the war, Robert!"
" Its worse, SVEN! Much worse!"
And I realised he was one who
knew + could remember. I understood how it completes a man + is
always there as a measuring device.

So when I heard from you it was
real + had a profound effect, because
we fought together, beyond the
fear barrier: for me anyway, in
a kind of ecstacy at Her's. the
thin silver thread of life held, in
all that violence — + the beautiful
people that came out of it! Odile,
whom you dont mention, still floats
before me in the candlelight +
smiled across the table on the
memorable birthday party they
gave you. Robert lighting my cigarette
with the candle flame to give
me his "smkings" / the old man
falling asleep. Madelaine busy, with
Ann-Marie watching.

Of all the photos the one that
moves me is the lane with their
cottage at La Rivière when Odile

Letter to Harry from Sven Berlin p2, 1994 (Jes Mainwaring)

came out to greet us + I drew my pistol.

I cannot tell you all that has happened to me, but send my Coat of Many Colours. published in June, which is the first volume of my Autobiography. The war is not mentioned much because of Lazarus, but this book is a story of a man's search for his soul + therefore, I have touched on the spiritual meaning at centre + am sure you will understand the brief mention of our friendship under fire: P216.

Thank you for Jean Brisset's Book, which is a real granery of information about the battles we fought. I will write to him but have no idea how he got my name, since I was an unknown soldier. I am pleased he included the press photo of us conferring with Robert.

I am glad you have restored your Medieval Church, I have a Madonna + Child carved in alabaster, 6ft high at present in the Lady Chapel of the Priory Church

Letter to Harry from Sven Berlin p3, 1994 (Jes Mainwaring)

at Christchurch, which, if you drive that way, I would like you to see. I lent it for their 900th Anno Celebrations: but they want to keep it, so I have said they can till the Spring. Otherwise I have not been a good Churchman because I have found so little inspiration among the clergy — except one Vicar in the New Forest who used to stride about like John the Baptist — but he has lost it in old age. I always worked best outside the orthodoxy: perhaps my work will balance this. I hope so.

Love to you both

SVEN...

On the phone I heard it as Peter Sears + said to myself: "Hill 112 was with Major Selfe!" Your letter confirms this. I remember that expedition as one of the toughest + he as a man of extraordinary understanding of his men. I was out on my own one night & frightened + he shared his slit trench — which probably saved my life.

you will be pleased to know that I hear the Notebooks & Journals you returned that Forms of Lazarus, one in the Imperial War Museum

Letter to Harry from Sven Berlin p4, 1994 (Jes Mainwaring)

Major Harry Mainwaring MC, February 1946 (Jes Mainwaring)

Lieutenant Colonel Harry Mainwaring MC MA, 2014

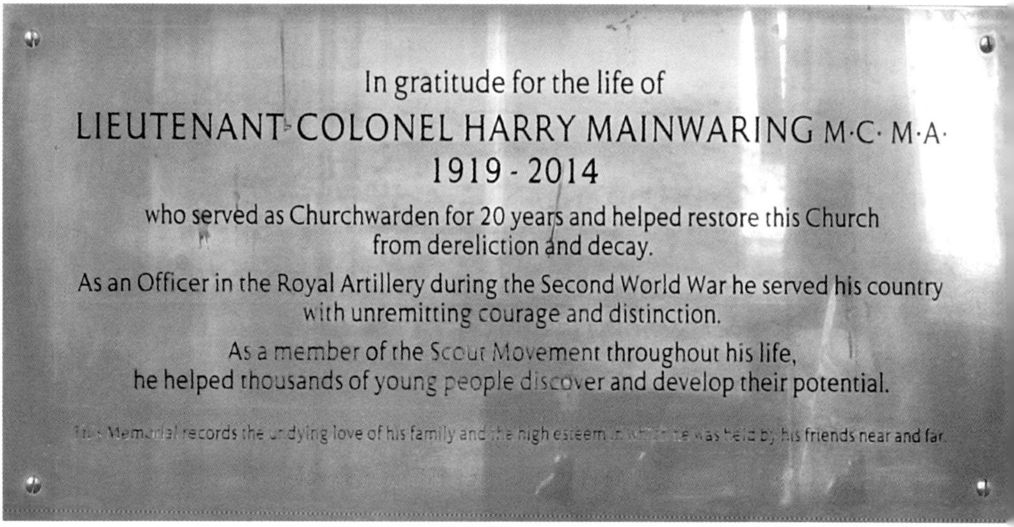

Memorial plaque in Church of St Nicholas, Denston, Suffolk, UK
(Jes Mainwaring)

moonlight at night. This enabled us to carry on for twenty-four hours a day, bringing our ammunition up to the dump and getting ready for the next stage. This was going to be the actual crossing of the Rhine. It was a hectic business that only slowed down a little while we waited until the day came for us to actually cross the river and move into the enemy heartland.

24 MARCH 1945 – CROSSING THE RHINE

A huge airdrop accompanied the actual attack on 23 March.

At the time I was in place for my liaison job with Monty's Phantom unit, similar to my earlier Phantom jobs in Normandy. It was quite thrilling really. All the messages and reports were coming through to the Phantom. From outside their marquee you could see the planes coming over, gliders going in to land, paratroopers dropping down. Sadly, we lost quite a number of our planes shot down in the attack.

The Germans had a terrific concentration of fire against us all along the other side of the river and it was far from easy going.

An interesting and unfortunate thing took place then, which I've never seen mentioned in any of the history books. The airborne troops who landed over on the far side of the river had to get through on their radio nets to our people across the river, especially the gunners who were controlling the covering fire. All our people who dropped made contact with us as planned from the north-east bank of the Rhine.

Something must have gone wrong with the radios of the American airborne forces landing further to our right. There was no contact. I suspect the wrong crystals had been fitted to the radios, giving incorrect frequencies in a similar way to the paratrooper communication problems at Arnhem.

The first contact made by US General Matthew B. Ridgway, who I came across later in Korea in 1950/1 with his men after they'd come down, was when he went over himself on a raft to get to their dropping zone to find them. They just hadn't made any radio contact at all. It was quite unusual and I've never heard any explanation.

This was the first time I'd been at Monty's Phantom when there was a full scale major offensive going in. It was very exciting to hear the results being reported at first hand. I suppose they were the only people who knew exactly what was going on over the river. Being part of this was very exhilarating.

In General Eisenhower's report about the north-west European campaign as supreme commander, he said that the three most decisive operations in that campaign were clear. First, the beaches. Of course, I wasn't there in those early days, we'd landed on 22 June when the beaches had already been cleared. The second one was the Falaise Pocket, in which I was very much involved. The third was these battles west of the Rhine in February to March 1945, before the actual crossing.

MARCH 1945 – PUSHING INTO GERMANY

Following the airdrops over the Rhine on 23 March, there were frantic efforts to get bridges across the river as swiftly as possible. And the next day, on 24 March, we crossed the River Rhine at Xanten. Once across, we advanced almost along the banks of the river down to Wesel.

Over the next three weeks we gradually moved ourselves slightly north of east going right across into the heart of Germany.

We pressed on from Wesel through Bocholt and, although names remain rather vague to me now, our route as I remember it was this. We moved on from Bocholt to Borken, to Coesfeld, and reached Munster. Munster is quite a big city, which we found in pretty bad shape when we reached it. I've been through all of them since the war when I was in BAOR between 1961 and 1965, and they have now, of course, all been rebuilt. From Munster on to Osnabruck, Lubbecke, to Minden, which I came to know well when I was at Bielefeld at HQ l(Br)Corps, to Nienberg, and then on to Celle.

Peter Selfe, our battery commander, was leaving the regiment on 24 April to go to Quetta to the staff college, so I was left temporarily in command of 9 Battery from this point until the end of hostilities.

We reached Celle somewhere around 24 April.

APRIL 1945 – THE HORROR OF BELSEN

Celle is a beautiful medieval town that had remained virtually unscathed and seemingly peaceful. There, we were switched northwards to head towards Hamburg.

Something like 15 miles north of Celle is a small town called Bergen. But when we got up there, I don't know how we were guided to it in the end, but we came upon the most awful concentration camp at Belsen. Nothing could have prepared us, however battle-hardened we had become, for what we found here.

Belsen was the most appalling sight. Perhaps from time to time one sees it on film, but nothing on celluloid can bring to the imagination how absolutely awful the place was.

There were literally living skeletons walking about. There was a pile of dead naked female bodies covering an area of probably half an acre. A vision of unutterable hell on earth, the very definition of the deepest suffering people are able to inflict on each other.

I think there were something like 60,000 people in the camp. Tragically, we ourselves were not able to do anything about treating anyone, for there were by then medical people who'd followed on very quickly.

It was truly terrible for us to helplessly stand by while there were still literally hundreds dying every day. They had been deliberately starved to death.

As fighting troops we had to go on, but whilst at Belsen it was all we could do as officers in the battery to stop our people gunning down the German prison staff who recognised no guilt and, surprisingly, were still around.

We were told of that awful bullying tyrant of a woman Irma Grese, who had made lampshades out of human skin. The most senior staff of the camp were tried and executed in December at the end of 1945.

The whole thing was beyond appalling. What happened in the camp after we left there I'm not quite sure, but when we left every one of us had learnt why we were fighting, what we were fighting for and what our enemy had done. (image 33)

HEAVEN FROM HELL

Two or three days after leaving the area of Belsen, my name was one of those pulled out of a hat for leave, so I was at last able to go home. I went off in a truck to Gennep, which had become the railhead for home leave.

I had seven wonderful days at home. It seemed like a visit to heaven after the terrible things we'd seen over the last ten months. And there I saw little Simon for the first time since I'd gone to Normandy. By this time he was 21 months old.

When I came back a week later, I was put in a truck at Gennep. I didn't know where the battery had got to by then, but we went back to Celle to pick up transport from our own units. Back in Celle I met the camp commandant of the forwarding outfit that had been set up as a sort of leave catchpoint.

He told me what had happened in Celle. All the leading citizens had been taken out to see the inhuman brutality and suffering inflicted in their name at Belsen. As well as this the military press photographers had taken pictures of those poor dying people in the camp, and hung prints of those photos on all the lampposts in Celle. Every citizen in Celle, who all claimed they knew nothing about the camp, was forced by the military to go round and see these photos.

They didn't want these people actually going into the camp itself, the prisoners' dignity had suffered enough. They will bear the marks of it for ever. Some of them did survive, but a great many continued to die there after the camp was liberated. It was the most awful experience of the whole of my life.

We ourselves had to go on to Soltau. I know that British medical people came in as well as a lot of volunteers from the London hospitals. I discovered much later in 2001, by an extraordinary coincidence, here in our tiny Suffolk village of Denston with fewer than 100 inhabitants, there are three of us with first-hand knowledge of Belsen.

One is a retired doctor, Alan MacAuslan, who went to Belsen as a volunteer from The Royal London Hospital and has written of his time there in the book *Darling Darling Meg...Belsen? Where's That?*, published in 1996 by the Pentland Press Ltd. Alan was in Belsen from 3 to 28 May 1945. He said in his book: 'On 28th May 1945 we returned to Britain, after twenty-six days in the real world.'

The other is Wally Twitchett, whose family have been in this village since the 1700s. He was in the Royal Military Police and was there when the original huts of the entire camp were burned down on 21 May.

The three of us were there at quite different periods. Alan MacAuslan told me that it was not until 1950 that the last of the internees were able to be repatriated from the new temporary buildings on the site of the original concentration camp of Belsen.

LOOTING REVEALED

I went on then from Celle in one of my own battery's vehicles to rejoin the battery. I can't remember exactly where we'd got to by then, but it was somewhere in the region of Soltau. As we went up from Soltau towards Hamburg, Buchholz is a name that hangs in my mind so I presume we must have got that far. As things were moving quite fast, I can't recall precise details of how we got there. The Germans were still fighting pretty hard with grim determination at this time, and one thing I remember distinctly was that somewhere along the road north of Soltau we'd been held up. We weren't in action there but we'd halted for some reason.

On this road we came across a farmhouse. The Germans had created a huge workforce of foreign slave workers, Russian prisoners-of-war, French citizens, all sorts of people they'd brought forcibly from the conquered countries to work for them in appalling near-starvation conditions.

A Russian prisoner-of-war slave worker at this farmhouse came up and beckoned to us to come down to the house. Nearly all German houses have cellars. The battery had moved fairly quickly whilst I'd been on leave and in that particular area most of the houses were undamaged. The Russian, wearing little more against the cold than a ragged worn shirt and a threadbare coat, indicated that we should go down to the cellar.

Down at the bottom of the stairs there was a passage with doors leading off, ending with a blank wall. We couldn't understand what the Russian was saying, but he indicated that we should 'attack' the wall to break through it. So I sent someone back to the vehicles to fetch pickaxes and so on, and we smashed our way through the wall.

Hidden behind it was a huge area half the size of the ground floor area above. I suppose it was 30' x 20' (9m x 6m) at least. And in there, oh my god, were piles of corn, cured pigs' carcasses hanging up. Food, plenty of food hidden from the hands of the starving slave workers. There were piles and piles of boxes of silk stockings from French towns. There were golden crosses from churches. There was all sorts of loot from occupied countries. I went to report this to our commanding officer, and he reported to our CAGRA.

The brigadier ordered us to go and inspect every one of these big farmhouses in the area. And we found that in each farmhouse a similar secret was concealed. At least half the cellar space below the house in every farmhouse we searched was similarly bricked up. Presumably the other half was kept for protection against bombing or shelling but also to maintain the deception. There were all these massive stores of food as well as rich pickings stolen by the Germans thieving in the occupied territories. I can't remember which farm I was in.

I had come from Belsen only a little up the road. I had seen for myself how inhumanely and brutally decent people had been treated there. I had just returned from a week of leave in the warmth of love and humanity at home in England. I became outraged beyond my normal levels of self-restraint when I uncovered these life saving stashes of food, wilfully hidden from their starving slaves through this deception by normal German people.

I was in the living room of one of these farmhouses. I smashed every darned thing I could find in it. Plates, chairs. I made a hell of a mess. I behaved like an absolute rampaging vandal. I don't suppose I would do that now but, at the time, it seemed the only thing to do to show them the consequences of what was done under the Nazis in the name of the German people. And to allow my own rage to work itself out.

I imagine looking at it now, calmly and many years later, they were doubtless protecting their own safety and acting under government orders. An excuse we later heard many times for many atrocities, but nevertheless in cold blood thinking of it after fifty years, I still feel a little ashamed of myself.

But I also think it was understandable.

MAY 1945 – UNCONDITIONAL SURRENDER

From that point to the actual end of the war in Europe, things moved pretty fast.

Hamburg didn't fall until 4 May, only four days before the fighting actually stopped and the war against Germany finally came to an end. We were switched over to the Luneburg Heide where Field Marshal Montgomery finally took the unconditional surrender of all German forces in the northern Europe theatre on 8 May 1945.

Before the fall of Hamburg, we moved forward from that farmhouse near Buchholz, across the Elbe at Lauenburg and then went round the eastern suburbs of Hamburg. Hamburg had been absolutely flattened by terrific bombing by the RAF some time before we got there.

From there we headed our way north-west round the northern outskirts of Hamburg and went up through a smallish, quite nice little town called Bad Bramstedt. The only thing I remember about that was that it had a very wide main street. Days were going by. We knew the fighting was going to stop on 8 May. We had actually been given word of that.

In the event, we could have advanced many miles further east. However, this was not permitted under Eisenhower's master plan agreed by the Allied governments. We had to wait for the Russians to make progress westwards to the predetermined area they were going to take over. So we, the British Army, didn't go very far to the east of Lubeck. Even so, we really could have swanned on because things were getting much easier now.

We reached the outskirts of Neumunster on the evening of 6 May and felt we needed to put on a show of force to make sure there was no nonsense. When we entered Neumunster at first light on 7 May, we drove the whole regiment, fairly well spaced apart with 50 or

60 yards between each vehicle, all the way round the major roads in Neumunster.

Twice.

Then they would think that there were more of us than there were.

AND THAT WAS WHERE WE REMAINED...

...until the regiment was disbanded some time in March 1946.

Once we were in Neumunster we were stationed in the former German artillery barracks, Artillerie Kaserne, and we were not allowed to fraternise with the Germans in any way.

6 ALL IS WELL ENDED

MAY 1945 – OCCUPATION

We still had our usual four batteries, and each battery had a different job to do. But in the meantime we were concerned about what might be about to happen, and I've never seen mention of this in any history of the war.

The Nazis had said earlier that whatever might happen some of them would never give up. They talked of forming resistance groups they called 'Werewolves'. They would be fanatical Nazis who would come out of the shadows, stalk us and shoot us up, and so on.

So, as we were not trained infantrymen we had to do an intensive course in infantry tactics, just as the war was over. We were trained up in the close urban tactics necessary to go and root out these groups when they might appear.

None ever did.

It was a waste of time really. They just gave up and that was it. Not a squeak out of them.

The main job the batteries had was to guard a leather factory down the road from the barracks. Into this place were herded 10,000 captured Nazis. Every single one of them was potentially a war criminal, and had to be cleared before they could be released. They all, of course, claimed they were not Nazis and knew nothing of any of their appalling activities over the previous years. It was incredible.

Every battery had one day in four guarding this factory, and for the remaining three days each battery was left to its own devices. Time seemed to pass fairly slowly after all the excitement that had gone before.

HIDDEN ARMS

One of the things we had to do immediately the war was finished while we were still in Neumunster was to seek out all the arms still in the hands of the civilian population, many of whom had only recently declared to be 'civilian'. An order was issued and promulgated by the military authorities to all the German households that any arms had to be given up.

I think they were given a week to hand them in. If any had not been handed in by then and were discovered, the owners would be taken into custody.

I went round with one of the field security chaps, who was a fluent German linguist. Old animosities surfaced when they were finally defeated as some of the Germans informed against each other. On one occasion a chap had been reported as having a weapon, so we knocked at the door and said we'd come to collect his weapon.

He said: "Search the place, I have nothing here."

To which the field security officer responded: *"Sie lügen, Mein Herr, Sie lügen."* ("You are lying, *Mein Herr*, you are lying.")

The German fellow looked terrified, and eventually led us round to his greenhouse lean-to behind the house and there, buried in the ground under the shelves for his plants, was a well-maintained and efficient looking rifle, all carefully wrapped and oiled.

So we took him off.

I don't know what happened to him after he was arrested, but I'm pretty sure he would have survived longer in prison than he would have done if he had played the Werewolf.

BACK TO 25 BATTERY

Earlier, I explained that when the regiment was split in two in January 1943, half went off to form 56 Medium and Heavy Training Regiment.

I had been moved over from the job of adjutant to form one of the two replacement batteries, in my case 25 Battery. But then Laurie Wass, who was senior to me, had been posted in from the 59th (Newfoundland) Heavy Regiment as commanding officer, with me staying on as battery captain. After CAGRA's massive series of demotions and the posting in of three new regular majors, I'd moved to 9 Battery as battery captain and Laurie Wass remained as battery captain in 25 Battery. Both of us served throughout the European campaign as battery captains.

By now Peter Selfe, my former battery commander, and Toby Welch, commanding officer of 25 Battery, who were both regular officers, had been posted to the Far East. In the last week in April Peter went to the staff college in Quetta.

As battery captain I had been placed temporarily in command of 9 Battery. When we got to Neumunster, I was promoted to the temporary rank of major and posted sideways to command 25 Battery as the replacement for Toby Welch.

In May 1945, no one knew that the war against Japan would end suddenly after the dropping of the atomic bombs in August only three months later.

For me to be posted back after almost two-and-a-half years to 25 Battery, the battery I had formed from scratch in January 1943, was a delightful experience. On the other hand, it was equally sad to leave the men I had served with throughout the Normandy campaign and then on into Holland and Germany. But it was wonderful to meet again the chaps I'd known then, most of whom were still with the battery, as well as its excellent sergeant-major.

He later came to visit my family and me after I'd been demobbed and we'd bought our house in Cambridge.

DISPLACED PERSONS CAMPS

Now the actual fighting was over, each of the battery commanders in Neumunster was given a specific task in dealing with the German population.

My particular task was to register all the 'displaced persons', all the people who had been taken from their own countries into Germany to work for the Germans.

In the end, we had a register of over 26,000 of these people, male and female. There were Norwegians, Danes, Dutch, Belgians, French, people from Estonia, Latvia, and Lithuania. There were Russians, people from almost every country you could think of conquered by the Germans were represented.

I had to go round to all the various camps. They had camps around, not within, Neumunster town, but well clear of it. The conditions were utterly appalling. What was, I thought, the most inhumane thing of all was that the Nazis had never provided them as far as I could see with any proper ablutions or proper lavatory arrangements. In several of the camps there were great heaps of ordure. Stinking, filthy. I do not want to distress anyone but it was absolutely horrifying. Disease, simply waiting to break out.

And these poor people when we registered them. Their clothing. The men maybe had a jacket and, if they were lucky, a shirt of some sort, trousers, and shoes although many had no socks. Certainly they seemed to have no underwear.

The women had only a dress. Luckily it was during mid- to late May, it was not cold, and the weather was pretty reasonable. But the women had no underwear, no stockings or socks.

One of the more distressing jobs I had to see to was particularly upsetting. They all had to be deloused. Of course, they were all in a pretty rough state and amongst them were a lot of Polish displaced persons. I had to go round with a spray and delouse hundreds of people.

The delousing was a very unpleasant job. You had to swoosh your spray thing up and down. It really was most undignified for these poor people, but it had to be done. It really was awful for all concerned.

Eventually, of course, the time came. They were all very anxious to get home. They were sent away in trainload after trainload from Neumunster station. We were simply ordered to put them on the trains, nationality by nationality. We had no idea of their ultimate destinations.

I saw that in 1989 there was a court case against a retired brigadier, who was chief of staff of V Corps in Italy or Austria at this time. He was accused by Count Tolstoy of being a war criminal, for sending people back to Russia. I don't know about us. We were sending liberated people back to their own countries everywhere. Russians, we assumed, wanted to go back to Russia. Whether they were going back to their deaths I just don't know now. We sent them back to their homes as we were instructed to do. I don't think at the time there was any thought of any problems. They were just so glad it was all over and they could go home.

LIFE AFTER SURRENDER

Conditions for the German civilians in Neumunster left them pretty short of everything, so black markets inevitably sprang up. We were on excellent field rations. Among them was a ration of twenty cigarettes a day. I didn't smoke, so I gave mine to my batman, good old Jock Flynn.

It seems that the 'dimps', the ends of partly smoked cigarettes, used to be gathered up into tobacco tins. The German locals were desperate enough for tobacco to be willing to pay an unbelievable 200 marks for a tin of dimps, worth £5 at the time. A lot of money. I believe a packet of twenty cigarettes went for at least £5 or even more. It seems that a lot of soldiers were selling these and getting themselves some extra money to send home. Not entirely commendable, it has to be said, but also not entirely manageable in that fairly tense environment.

Very few men had gone home by the time the regiment was disbanded in March 1946. To keep the chaps occupied until they became due for demobilisation, I decided that the best thing to do to keep them from getting bored and restless was to keep them active.

Sport usually does a good job at this.

I didn't know what the other batteries were getting up to, but it seemed to me we could create a sports field behind the barracks. It's quite a job to make a decent sports field.

We made a very good one in the end, with track activities and football and so on. The other batteries were a bit envious and came over asking to have a share in the use of it. I had then to work out a timetable so people could share what we'd done.

Horse-riding seemed like another engaging activity that would absorb a bit of time if you could find the horses. Curiously, it just so happened that in this particular former German army artillery barracks there was a covered riding school and an open riding school. Which meant we acquired about twenty-six horses I remember, beautiful horses, Hungarian I believe.

The second-in-command of the regiment, Freddie Hewitt, happened to be an expert horseman. He'd done the army riding course. Those of us who wanted to ride, and I was particularly keen, he put through what he said was something pretty similar to the official army riding course. After that, every day for months I was on horseback somewhere, going round the outskirts of Neumunster or jumping in the riding school, indoor or outdoor, depending on the weather. I remember jumping a pretty high fence, about 5'6" (1.7m), and I have never forgotten the almighty wallop I gave myself. I wasn't properly seated, all over the place. Anyway, it was great fun and certainly helped to pass the time.

THE TRIAL OF PIERRE LAVAL

In August 1945, three months after the war in Europe was finished, the war against the Japanese was over too. A few days' leave was given to the smallish number of people who wished to go to Paris.

We drove all the way through in one of the regiment's vehicles. Petrol was not that easily available, but we got there anyway. We stayed in the King George the Fifth Hotel, and for a couple of nights I stayed with Robert Duguey, who was a barrister and back in Paris.

He took me to hear some of the trial of Pierre Laval, who was head of the Vichy government that wilfully collaborated with the German occupying regime. His contribution to the Nazi reign of terror in France included the organisation of the deportation of French Jews to the concentration camps to be murdered. He also provided slave labourers who were deported to Germany, some of whom were the survivors we had only recently been involved in returning to their homes.

Laval was subsequently found guilty and executed by firing squad in October 1945.

WHOM AGE SHALL NOT WEARY

Some time after I returned to 25 Battery, the regiment was required to send its guns away. The fighting was over, the guns were to be returned back to store, and we had to get the guns ready. I am not sure where they were taken in the first instance, although it was most likely to have been Hamburg, for onward transmission to the UK. As I've always been a bit of a romantic, I thought to myself: The guns in the Royal Artillery are our colours. We do not have colours in the same way as infantry regiments. The guns *are* our colours, and we were losing them.

It was extremely unpopular at the time and everybody thought it was a waste of time, but I decided that when the guns were to go at the crack of dawn one morning, I'd form the whole of the battery up on parade.

We would be properly dressed, we'd have our arms, and we would present arms, the highest possible salute to the guns as they were driven away.

Before the actual ceremony, I read out the casualty list of all the people in 25 Battery who'd been killed or wounded. Every one of them I knew from 1943 and I read this list out, loud and clear.

By then men from the other three batteries in the barracks were watching us from the windows of their blocks. When the guns had left and we had all gone back indoors, my chaps in 25 Battery were immensely proud.

There was tangible disappointment amongst the other batteries that they had not done as we had. I was quite surprised to find many of the other batteries' officers saying they wished they had done what we did. Feeling rather bloody-minded, I thought this was the only thing we could do.

We had lost these men killed, and many others who had been wounded. We had seen the way these men had died. It made us realise that what we had been fighting for was a peaceful future and those killed had given their all. They had given up their future for a future for others. At that particular time those thoughts were pretty well up in my mind. (image 34)

DISBANDMENT OF THE REGIMENT

Time went by and eventually the regiment was very sadly disbanded. Those of us whose demob date had not yet come were then posted. The 'other ranks' were sent off to various other regiments, and pending demob, all the officers were attached to the 63rd Anti-Tank Regiment RA (Oxfordshire Yeomanry). There we passed the time of day really not doing very much. Sometimes we went walking on the cliffs near Travemunde, or going out to lunch at the officers' club. It was all rather time-wasting, but we had no choice but to just wait.

The war in the Far East hadn't finished and those of us still in Europe were affected by the number of our release group. Reinforcements or replacements were required for the Far East to continue the war against Japan. They were needed in order to allow those out there who'd been out of the UK for four years or more to return home on leave under the Python scheme.

The government had decided that those serving in Europe with release group numbers of twenty-seven or above were now liable to be posted to the Far Fast. The group number you were given depended upon your age and date of joining the forces, whether voluntarily, as I had, or conscripted.

I breathed a sigh of relief, because my own release group was number twenty-six, and this meant that I would be released from Europe in due course.

MILITARY CROSS AND MENTIONS IN DESPATCHES

In August 1945 I had notification that I had been Mentioned in Despatches, which Peggy and my father were very pleased about.

Then later, in January 1946, I had another notification that I had a second Mention in Despatches. And then I received yet another notification.

It had also been decided I was going to be awarded the Military Cross, like my father in 1917. So that was something to be very proud of and certainly Peggy and my father were happy.

I never saw the citations for my Mentions in Despatches so I don't know what they were for, but I understand that when you're 'mentioned', there had been some fairly heartfelt recommendation. Sometimes you might have been recommended for an MC, but whatever you did had not been thought enough to warrant a decoration of that level and been downgraded to a Mention. So I'll never know. I'd had a pretty hectic time overall, and I was jolly glad to be so honoured.

But mostly, I was jolly glad to still be alive at the end of it all.

7 AND IN THE MORNING

SPRING 1946 – A DECISION OF CONSCIENCE

Going back to the summer of 1945, after the war was over, as part of the demob process they started what was called 'Class B Release'. That was for undergraduates who had not been regular soldiers to enable them to go back to university to finish the degree course they'd started before the war.

I'd been up at Queens' College, Cambridge. I had intended in my second year, which had so far not happened, to read Theology. After the end of the war with the Class B Release coming along, I had the offer to return to Queens' to take up the Theological Tripos.

However by then I had been through the European campaign and been involved in killing in my OP and other duties by frequently calling down fire on the enemy, and by closer contact.

The sixth commandment says: Thou shalt not kill.

I no longer felt it was right to take up the Class B Release. I hadn't lost any of my Christian faith, but I didn't feel it was right to go on to become a parson.

So I didn't accept the offer, and waited until my normal time came to go out under what was called Class A Release with my Group 26, which eventually came on 17 April 1946.

So I went home.

HOME AGAIN

It was wonderful to get back to Peggy and Simon. Shortly after the end of April, we went up to Altrincham for a brief visit to my father. Whilst we were there my father gave me the most wonderful present I had ever received from him, or anyone.

It was a beautiful book entitled *An Introduction to Heraldry*, clad in red leather with the title embossed in gold leaf on the front cover, and gold leaf to the edges of the vellum pages. Having been a design engineer, he was both an artist and a wonderful draughtsman. The book was painstakingly written, entirely by hand, in my father's particular style of meticulous italicised script, and illustrated with coats-of-arms drawn in fine detail in the glowing colours of Indian inks, each one of which could be covered by an old silver sixpenny piece.

Prefaced with a moving personal dedication on answering the country's call to arms, I realised he had undertaken this task throughout the war from the day I volunteered until my return.

One of the consequences of remaining and not taking the offer of Class B Release was that I had been able to live very sparingly and save most of my pay. When I eventually got home and we were looking for somewhere to live when I went back to Queens', I had saved enough for us to be able to buy our house in Fen Ditton, Cambridge. So those extra months, though they meant longer separation from Peggy and Simon, helped us to become financially independent after the war, which was an important thing.

GOOD OMENS

Going forward now in time to 1950, I had gone back into the army as a regular officer with the rank of major. I was rather thinking it would now be a fairly safe and secure career. Having completed my tripos at

Queens', it seemed to be appropriate for me to join the Royal Army Education Corps (RAEC). I hoped here I may be able to help people achieve the potential they might be capable of. I had seen enough of a world where too many people had been led away from such a course.

Within months I was unexpectedly and reluctantly sent out to the Korean War. Myself and another officer, Major John Grimsey MC, were selected as it was felt only decorated RAEC officers should be sent to an active war zone as their fighting credentials were already established. In the event, I produced the army newspaper, now archived with the Imperial War Museum.

I went from home in Cambridge down to Southampton to the troopship without knowing how long I'd be away. I left home for the last evening train from Cambridge and slept on one of the benches in the waiting room at Liverpool Street Station for a time, so that I could get over to Waterloo early in the morning. I got on the first underground train to Waterloo and, unbelievably, found myself sitting next to one of my old sergeants from the battery, Sergeant Harding. He was now working for the Post Office at the Mount Pleasant sorting office. We had a long chat but eventually he had to say goodbye and get off.

When I went to exchange my railway warrant at Waterloo, who should the clerk behind the glass window be but Bombardier Johnny Griggs who'd been our pay bombardier in the battery. Finally, I got on board the troopship, the *Empire Medway*, and telephones were installed on board so we could ring up home before the troopship sailed.

To cap it all, whilst I was actually speaking to Peggy on the phone, along the deck came Driver Vickerson. Although he was a coal miner now, he had still been called back off the reserve.

When Peggy and I were first married and we had those rooms in Tillingham, near the battery in St Lawrence, it was Driver Vickerson who used to bring round my daily rations in the ration wagon.

So there were three people connected with my time in the 53rd Heavy Regiment during the war that I saw on the very day that I was going off to Korea. That was some solace when I was feeling pretty miserable, and I thought all of this had to be a good omen.

AND FINALLY – SOME TIME LATER

A WEDDING IN DENMARK

Not long ago Peggy and I were writing pretty vociferous letters to the local press against the damage caused by straw-burning in Suffolk.

The phone rang one evening, and in a very broad Suffolk accent a voice asked if I was the Mainwaring who'd been in the 53rd Heavy Regiment and of course I said that I was. The caller said: "This is Driver Davy. You came up to Kolding in Denmark to be a witness at my wedding when I married my wife Irena."

That was a wonderful thing, because Driver Davy had been detached from the regiment with his ammunition lorry to help take forward the stores. These had to be sent forward 400 miles from Arromanches to keep the forward troops supplied before the port of Antwerp was taken.

Whilst Davy was on this job he'd met a Norwegian girl who was acting as a Norwegian liaison officer. She was attached to the Women's ATS (Auxiliary Territorial Service) and they'd fallen for each other. So when the fighting was over he'd kept in touch with her. They'd arranged for their wedding up at Kolding in Denmark, which is not far north of Flensburg, so the commanding officer sent me up there to act as a formal witness at their wedding at the British Consulate.

Billy Davy lived in Bury St Edmunds, only 10 miles from where we lived. So we went round to see them and had a very pleasant evening. They showed us their wedding photos which including one of me with his wife and her sister.

GIFTS FROM COPENHAGEN

On another occasion during the autumn of 1945, several of us went up on a very brief leave to Copenhagen. By then the shops had become full of all the goodies that were still rationed in England. So I got one or two presents for Peggy and at the same time I ordered a huge Danish blue cheese. I had it all packed up and sent off through the mail to Langford. The postman duly brought this parcel round and knocked on the door: "I've got something here that doesn't smell very nice. It's come all the way from Denmark."

When Peggy opened the parcel there was this magnificent cheese, smelling intensely but wonderfully edible, and very welcome in those still-rationed times.

I will end this reminiscence here. I've no doubt there are hundreds of episodes of my time in the European campaign and the rest of my time in the army during the war that I've forgotten. Perhaps they might come out in conversation with my family at some other time. But this is the end of these reminiscences for the time being.

APPENDIX

Letter to Harry from Sven Berlin

22 November 1994

Dear Harry,

"Le recherche du temps perdu!" And with it an artillery barrage of emotion: feeling, clear visual memory, and a deep stirring in the heart that was frightening, to get your phone call and letter with the book and photographs. I had no idea your friendship with Robert and his family was so complete. I think I sent him Lazarus (I Am Lazarus by Sven Berlin, Gollancz, 1961) at the time but that is all. Since writing it, I have had to put the experience away to be able to deal with the difficulties and battles of another kind.

I did not take part in the Remembrance this year, because only those old men in suits and berets and medals knew the horror and depth of suffering and love. They were either silent or inarticulate and broke down afterwards. But those who watched had no idea. I could not have stood the pressure. I thought Lazarus had done it for me. Robert Graves, when he was advising me about a tragedy in my own life, looked very seriously at me when I said "It's almost as bad as the war, Robert."

"It's worse Sven! Much worse!" I realised he was one who knew and could remember. I understood how it completes a man and is always there as a measuring device.

So when I heard from you it was real and had a profound effect, because we fought together, <u>beyond the fear barrier</u>: for me anyway, in a kind of ecstasy at Flers. The thin silver thread of life held, in all that violence – and the beautiful people that came out of it! Odile, whom you don't mention, still floats before me in the candlelight and smiles across the table on the memorable birthday party they gave you. Robert lighting my cigarette with the candle flame to give me his 'sinkings'! The old man falling asleep. Madeleine busy, with Anne Marie watching. Of all the photos, the one that moves me is the lane with their cottage at La Riviere when Odile came out to greet us and I drew my pistol.

I cannot tell you all that has happened to me but send my Coat of Many Colours, published in June, which is the first volume of my Autobiography. The war is not mentioned much because of Lazarus, but this book is a story of a man's search for his soul and therefore I have touched on the spiritual meaning at the centre and am sure you will understand the brief mention of our friendship under fire, page 216.

Thank you for Jean Brisset's book, which is a real a granary of information about the battles we fought. I will write to him, but have no idea how he got my name since I was an unknown soldier. I am pleased he included the press photo of us conferring with Robert.

I am glad you have restored your Medieval Church. I have a Madonna and Child carved in alabaster, 6 feet high, at present in the Lady Chapel of the Priory Church at Christchurch, which if you drive that way, I would like you to see. I lent it for their 900th Anno Celebrations, but they wanted to keep it, so I have said they can till the spring. Otherwise, I have not been a good churchman because I have found so little inspiration among the clergy – except one vicar in the New Forest who was who used to stride about like John the Baptist – but he has lost it in old age. I always worked best outside the orthodoxy: perhaps my work will balance this. I hope so.

Love to you both
Sven.

On the phone I heard it as Peter Sears, and said to myself. "Hill 112 was with Major Selfe." Your letter confirms this. I remember that expedition as one of the toughest and he as a man of extraordinary understanding of his men. I was out on my own one night and frightened, he shared his slit trench- which probably saved my life.

You will be pleased to know that I hear the Notebooks and Journals you returned that formed Lazarus are in the Imperial War Museum.

I hope my book won't bore you: it is of artists who are not so generous as soldiers.

(Sven Berlin 22 November 1994)

ACKNOWLEDGEMENTS

The greatest acknowledgment goes to Harry, Peggy and their generation for the sacrifices they willingly made to enable the future we have inherited rather than sink into 'the abyss of a new Dark Age'. My thanks to Lieutenant Colonel Peter Thompson, Catherine Buchanan, David Taylor, Peter Gilmour and Jerry Hewitt for their support and encouragement. Particular thanks go to my brother Simon for his contributions over the years, and very special thanks to Hazel for accepting the amount of time it has taken. I would also like to thank Tara Moran and Harriet Fielding at Pen & Sword Books for recognising the significance of the story in today's world, and for bringing it into production.

AUTHOR DETAILS

Jes Mainwaring is primarily an architect rather than writer (albeit these share common elements), and an unpublished poet. Jes names his father Harry as the true author as he lived the story. Jes prompted and enabled Harry to make an audio recording of that story while it was still 'living history'. Since the spoken word does not read so well in word-for-word transcript, Jes edited the script to make it more reader friendly whilst adding Harry's occasional further recollections and Peggy's civilian insights. Initially Jes made a few hardback copies by hand for family under the title Bow and Arrow Man, but encouragement from various directions has led to this point of publication.